HOW MUCH
AND
HOW MANY?

HOW MUCH & HOW MANY

THE STORY OF WEIGHTS AND MEASURES

REVISED EDITION
by

JEANNE BENDICK

FRANKLIN WATTS | 1989
NEW YORK | LONDON | TORONTO | SYDNEY

FRONTIS: A MODEL OF AN ELEVENTH-CENTURY
CHINESE WATER CLOCK DRIVE MECHANISM.

Library of Congress Cataloging-in-Publication Data
Bendick, Jeanne.
How much and how many? : the story of weights and measures / by
Jeanne Bendick. — Rev. ed.
p. cm.
Includes index.
Summary: Compares and explains weights and measures throughout the
world as well as the history of many current standards.
ISBN 0-531-10679-9
1. Weights and measures—Juvenile literature.   2. Weights and
measures—History—Juvenile literature.   [1. Weights and measures—
History.]   I. Title.
530.8—dc19   QC90.6.B46   1989   88-38065   CIP   AC

HOW MUCH
AND
HOW MANY?

HOW MUCH
—— AND ——
HOW MANY?

If you say that something is very big, that doesn't tell you much about it. Is it bigger than an elephant? Bigger than a house? Bigger than a baseball diamond?

If you say that something is very heavy, that doesn't tell much either. Is it heavier than a rock? Heavier than a log? Heavier than a barrel of apples?

To tell how big or how heavy something is, you have to compare it with something else. Measuring is comparing. So is weighing.

If you say that there are a lot of houses on the block, or a lot of apples in a barrel, you aren't telling anything specific, either. To do that, you have to compare in a different way. You have to match things with numbers to tell how many.

Everything you eat and wear; live in and ride in; the words in your books and newspapers; the pictures on a television screen and the symbols on a computer screen; the rain, wind, and snow; the earth, sea, and stars—all have been measured, weighed, or counted in some way. The ways of measuring and counting all these things are almost endless. Sometimes a thing can be weighed or measured in a dozen different ways.

Even from the earliest times, people had ways of measuring. There were certain things they had to know, such as how much land did a farmer have to plant? How much cloth did it take to make a dress? How much meat could a hunter trade for how much grain?

At first, ways of figuring these things were simple. People used the most convenient measures— themselves. The length of a foot or a stride was a measure. So was the span of a hand or the thickness of a finger, or a handful of one thing for a handful of something else.

But as civilizations grew, these ways of measuring weren't adequate anymore. How could a foot be used as a measure when one person's foot was so much longer than another's? Hands and fingers were different sizes, too. And who decided how long a measuring stick should be?

As soon as people began doing business on a large scale, they needed better ways of measuring. When they began building towns and ships, dividing land, and trading with people they didn't know and sometimes never even met, the early ways of measuring had to be improved. It was important for a trader between Babylon and Jerusalem to know that a bolt of cloth in one city was equal to a bolt of cloth in the other. If a king wanted his palace walls built 50 cubits high, he didn't expect each workman to measure off those cubits in the old way—from the tip of his elbow to the end of his middle finger. He wanted the walls to be the same height all around. There had to be standard measures that were the same everywhere.

Measuring came before weighing. It's simple to measure an amount of something—the length of a foot or an arm, a gourd full of water, or an eggshell full of grain. Weight, as a separate way of measuring, was harder to figure out.

An early way of thinking about weight probably had to do with the amount a person could carry. But although someone could carry a very big bundle of straw, a person could carry only a couple of rocks or a small hunk of iron. And although a bucket of berries was light, the same bucket filled with sand was heavy. Actually, people weren't measuring weight at all but size or number. They didn't know how much rocks weighed, only that two medium-size ones were enough to carry.

The idea that weight itself, quite separate from size, could be a way of measuring took more time to develop. At first, people compared weight by balancing small objects, one in each hand, and guessing whether one was heavier or if the two weighed about the same. About seven thousand years ago, the Egyptians devised a crude scale—a stick hanging by a cord tied around its middle. The objects to be weighed were hung on other cords, one at each end of the stick. If their weights were about equal, the stick stayed parallel to the ground.

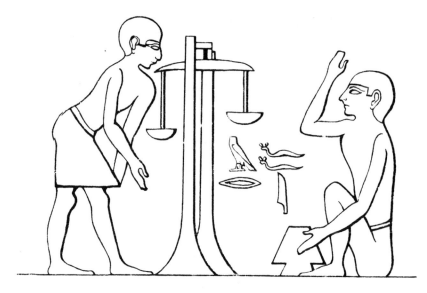

Ancient Egyptian balance (about 2500 B.C.).
Shown are two jewelers at work. As the
cross-beam balances, the man squatting
on the right raises his hand.

Ancient
Mesopotamian
weights

If one object was heavier, the stick dipped at the end.

By about 3000 B.C., the Egyptians were making small weights out of stone. This was a big advance because the weights themselves were nothing anyone wanted. They were used to represent amounts of other things that did have value.

The ancient Babylonians, Egyptians, Greeks, and Romans had hundreds of different weights to meet the needs of their thriving civilizations. The same weights were used by everyone. There were common weights for honey and other foods, for medicines, and for metals and precious stones. There were also standard measures for buildings, for land, and for cloth.

There are still groups of people in the world who do not have elaborate systems of weights and measures simply because they don't need them. In remote places where business is done by trading one object for another, and where the land and food belong to everyone, there isn't any reason to bother.

In ancient times a weight or measure that was used in one country was often later adopted by others through trade or invasion. Roman weights, measures, and coins spread throughout Europe and western Asia, England, and Africa when the Romans conquered and occupied those lands. But gradually, through mistakes in copying and figuring, the standards became so confused that many of them dropped out of use. By the sixteenth century most of the people in Europe had returned to the old body measurements.

We still use some of these today. In England,

people still use the *digit,* which is the width of a finger, or 3/4 of an inch. (A single number is also called a *digit.*)

A *hand* is 4 inches, the width of a good-sized human hand. The hand is still used for measuring horses, as it was in the earliest trading days, thousands of years ago. The height of a horse, measured in hands, is the distance from the ground to the top of the horse's shoulder.

The *span* is another measure that started with the hand. It began as the distance from the end of the thumb to the end of the little finger when the fingers were spread out. A span is about 9 inches. It may also be measured as the width of two palms.

The *inch* started as a hand measurement, too. At first, it was the width of a man's thumb. Then it was measured in grains of barley—three in a row. Edward II of England made this law in the fourteenth century. "The length of an inch," he said, "shall be equal to three grains of barley, dry and round, placed end to end lengthwise."

The *foot* was always a common measure. In ancient times, it was quite a bit more than 12 inches. Feet must have become smaller when people took to wearing fancy sandals because the Greeks measured a foot at only 11½ inches. Archaeologists were able to figure out the length of the foot the Greeks used by taking thousands of measurements of Greek buildings. The Romans spread this short-foot measurement all through Europe. The 12-inch foot is standard only in English-speaking countries. In other places, a foot may be any length from 11 to 14 inches.

The *pace* was another common measure. It was about 5 feet—the length of a complete step counted from the time one foot left the ground until the same foot was put down again. Roman soldiers, marching across the countries they conquered, paced off the miles as they went. A thousand paces of the Roman soldiers made up a mile, just a little less than the modern mile, which is 5,280 feet. Some of the old Roman mile markers are still scattered around Europe to prove it. Now we measure a pace as either 2½ or 3 feet, the length of a single step.

The *yard* seems to have sprung up in several different places. In northern Europe, it was the length of the belt the Anglo-Saxons wore. In the southern countries, it was the length of a double cubit. A cubit is 18 inches. At the beginning of the twelfth century, Henry I of England is said to have fixed the yard as the distance from his nose to the thumb of his outstretched arm.

All through history, most standards of weight and measure have been fixed not by parliaments or houses of congress but by the rulers of countries or the chieftains of tribes. Most common measures in the so-called English or customary system have come down through the centuries without significant changes since the time of the Saxons. There is only about 1/100 of an inch difference between the earliest standard yard and the present one.

Ancient weights and measures were invented as they were needed and discarded when more practical ones came along. Once the yard was standardized, there was no need to measure a length of cloth around the elbow, so the measure called an "ell" disappeared. Modern coins are worth the amount stamped on them instead of the actual value of the metal they contain. There is no use now for the weights that coins were compared with to see if their value was true.

Today, goods are traded all over the world, so it's important to have worldwide standards. Land and sea areas must be measured exactly so that sailors and travelers everywhere can depend on their maps. Scientists and printers, doctors and pharmacists, engineers and astronauts all need exact standards so they can work easily with one another even though they may speak different languages.

Every trade, science, and profession has its own system of weights and measures. They are the "language" in which the work of the world is done.

Here are some things to remember about weights and measures.

UNITS AND STANDARDS

There is a difference between units and standards.

A *unit* is the given value, quantity, or size of a weight or measure. A unit is a unit only because the law says so. A yard is 36 inches only because the law says so. A meter is 100 centimeters only because the law says so. This is true of the pound and the pint, the kilogram, the liter, or any other legal weight or measure.

A *standard* is the actual, physical reproduction

of a unit. The yard is a unit of length, but a standard yard is a bronze bar with fine lines engraved in it exactly 36 inches apart on gold studs set in the bar. All yards are measured from a standard yard. For a long time a standard meter was a platinum and iridium bar exactly 39.37 inches long. All meters were measured from this.

As scientists found more precise ways of measuring, the standards had to become more precise. Now the meter is usually measured in wavelengths of light, given off from a lamp burning the gas krypton. Exactly 1,650,163.73 of these wavelengths equal a meter. Once there were only thirty standard meters in the world. Now a krypton lamp, which can be used anywhere under controlled conditions, serves the purpose. The old standard meters have become historical treasures.

At the end of the twelfth century, Richard I of England made the first law requiring actual standards for capacity, which is the amount a container will hold, and for length. These standards were made of iron and were kept by sheriffs and magistrates in different parts of the country. If a tradesman were suspected of giving short measure, his containers or yardstick could be compared with the standards.

When actual standards were first made, no two were exactly alike. But nobody could see a difference of 1/100 of an inch, and the standard was never used so precisely that it really mattered. But today, a difference of 1/100 of an inch could prevent precision machinery from working properly.

Just because he needed a cylinder so accurately cut that steam could not escape around a piston working inside it, James Watt could not build a full-size steam engine from his model for ten years. He had to wait until someone invented a machine that could bore the cylinder exactly right.

At the U.S. National Bureau of Standards, industrial and commercial standards of length and mass are compared often, to be sure they are accurate. The adjustments on the machine that compares standards of length are so delicate that the machine can detect a difference of less than a millionth of an inch. A millionth of an inch is the amount that a fly bends a steel bar by sitting on it.

DIVIDING UNITS

Units can be divided in a number of ways:

Decimally, which means into tenths. The decimal system was used by the ancient Egyptians and Chinese. The metric system is a decimal-based system.

Duodecimally, which means into twelfths. This method was used by the Romans. They divided the foot into 12 inches, the pound into 12 ounces, and the year into 12 months.

Binarily, which means into halves, then quarters, and so on. This was the Hindu way.

Sexagesimally, which means division by 60. This was the ancient Bablyonian way. Time and circles are still divided like this.

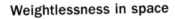

WEIGHT AND MASS

Weight is the strength of the pull of gravity on any object. *Mass* is the actual quantity of matter or material in that object.

Mass does not change, unless the object is moving very, very fast—almost as fast as the speed of light. Except for atomic particles, none of the solid things we measure moves that fast.

Weight can change. Gravity pulls from the center of the earth. The farther away an object is from the center of a massive body, the less it weighs. That's why astronauts out in space are weightless.

Weightlessness in space

If you took a sack of flour that weighed 100 pounds at sea level up a 20,000-foot mountain, it would weigh only 99 pounds, 13 ounces. The same sack of flour would weigh more at the North Pole than at the equator because the earth is slightly flatter at the poles, so a sack at the North Pole is nearer to the earth's center.

The weight of the sack of flour might change, but it would still contain the same amount of flour. Its mass has not changed. So instead of using weight as a standard, we use mass. People often use the word "weight" in place of the word "mass." Usually, weight and mass are about the same.

VOLUME

Volume is the measurement of the space occupied by anything. But while mass always remains the same, volume can change. If you beat the white of an egg, its volume changes quite a bit. It takes up much more space than it did before you beat it, even though the mass—the actual amount of egg white—is the same.

Weight, mass, volume, length, width, and height are measured all over the world, but there are different ways of measuring them. Many English-speaking countries use some variety of the English or customary system. Most of the world uses the metric system.

To avoid confusion, most countries have agreed to use the metric system as a standard when dealing with each other. The *kilogram* is the metric system's unit of mass. The standard kilogram is a cylinder of platinum and iridium weighing 2.2046 pounds at sea level. The pound of the English system is measured from that.

The yard and the pound are units of the customary system. But the standards for them are measured from the meter and the kilogram.

────────── SYSTEMS WITHIN SYSTEMS ──────────

Within the customary system there are other systems of measuring.

The *avoirdupois* (av-er-dew-POYZ) system is used for all commodities except precious metals and precious stones. These have their own system, called *troy weight*. Medicines are measured in *apothecaries' weight*. Avoirdupois is a French word meaning "goods of weight."

The avoirdupois system is divided again, into *dry measure* and *liquid measure*. Dry measure—a bushel or a peck, for example—is used for measuring items such as grain, fruit, and vegetables. Liquid measure—perhaps a pint or a gallon—is used for all liquids. Sometimes, liquid measures are used for dry items, too. You might get quarts or pints of berries or ounces of almost anything. Dry measure is never used for liquids in the United States, but sometimes it is used this way in England. Back in the fifteenth century, Henry VII of England, who set the first legal units of weight and measure, said, "Eight pounds do make a gallon of wine, and eight gallons of wine do make a bushel."

Linear measure is the measure of length. A plain ruler or a meter stick gives you linear measure—the length of a football field or the distance between bases on a baseball diamond. Linear distance may be given in customary or metric units.

Square measure is a system of units for measuring area. If you are measuring the living room floor for a rug, square measure will tell you the size of the area that has to be covered.

Cubic measure refers to volume or capacity. If you were a wholesale grocer who wanted to know what size carton you would need to hold fifty boxes of cereal, you would use cubic measure to solve the problem.

THE METRIC SYSTEM

Every civilized country in the world is either obliged by law or may voluntarily use the metric system of weights and measures.

Even in countries such as the United States, where the customary system is usual, the metric system is used for scientific and engineering purposes, for athletic events, in photography, and with firearms. These countries also use the two basic metric standards, the meter and the kilogram, to measure standard yards and pounds. Someday the metric system will probably be used everywhere.

The metric system was invented by the French in 1790, following the French Revolution. It was part of a plan for a new beginning—a whole new social and economic life in France, without any ties to the past. So a group of scientists got together to figure out a new system of weights and measures.

Street signs in Lakewood, Colorado, with
elevation measured in feet and meters

The meter, the basic unit of length, was originally supposed to be one ten-millionth part of the distance from the North Pole to the equator. But in the eighteenth century instruments were not as accurate as they are today, so there was a measurement error. By the time scientists discovered the mistake, the length of the meter was so well established that it was kept as it was, equal to 39.37 inches.

When the French invented the metric system, systems of weights and measures in the surrounding European countries were in great confusion. Every town or local government had its own variation of the system in use and there were no standards, so they welcomed this organized way of doing things. Actually, the slowest country to bring the metric system into common use was France itself, where it did not become popular for another forty years.

The English-speaking countries were satisfied with their system and didn't see any reason to change it. At the beginning of the nineteenth century, John Quincy Adams tried to persuade Congress to make the metric system the official system of weights and measures for the United States. It was a good idea, but it didn't get far. In 1866, the U.S. Congress made use of the metric system legal where it was found to be more convenient, but it still has not come into general use.

One thing that makes the metric system simple is that it is a decimal system and so it uses multiples of ten. And it is logical. There is a direct relationship of the units of length, weight, and capacity to one another.

The unit of length is the *meter.* A meter is 39.37 inches long.

The unit of mass is the *kilogram.* (*Kilo* means "thousand," so the word means "a thousand grams.")

Here is how the scientists decided on the mass of the kilogram: First, they made a cube with each side 1/10 of a meter long. This was a cubic decimeter (*decimeter* means 1/10 of a meter). They called the cubic decimeter the *liter* and decided that it would be the unit of volume. Then they decided that the amount of pure water that would fill this cubic centimeter would be the unit of mass, the kilogram.

It's easy to figure the value of any weight or measure in the metric system. Unlike the customary system, in which the weights and measures have names that don't give any clue to their value, the names of the units in the metric system tell you exactly what they are.

There are six prefixes that can be attached to any unit, and each of these prefixes refers to a number.

MILLI means 1/1000 (one one-thousandth)
CENTI means 1/100 (one one-hundredth)
DECI means 1/10   (one tenth)
DEKA means   10   times
HECTO means   100 times
KILO means   1000 times

Any of these prefixes attached to meter, gram, or liter tells you the exact value of the unit. A kilogram, for example, is 1,000 grams, and a hecto-gram is 100 grams. A milliliter is 1/1000 of a liter.

When the measurements are for scientific use it is often necessary to multiply or divide the basic units by more than a thousand. For that, there are other prefixes.

MYRIA means   10,000 times
MEGA means   1,000,000 (one million) times
MICRO means 1/1,000,000 of a part
                  (a micron is a millionth of a meter)
NANO means   one-billionth part
PICO means   one-trillionth part

A billionth or a trillionth part of a meter might seem too small to measure anything, but these mea-surements are useful when working with light waves or X-rays. In the customary system there is no standard unit smaller than an inch. There is no standard unit larger than a mile. You can see why scientists the world over use the metric system.

The metric system isn't only for science. It is also used to measure all kinds of dry goods and materials and for building and engineering. A me-ter is about 10 percent longer than a yard. The old English yard, which was abandoned in 1439, was 39.66 inches, almost exactly the same as the me-ter of today.

Centimeters and millimeters are used instead of inches in constructing machinery; in making fur-niture; and in measuring book and paper sizes. A centimeter is about 2/5 of an inch and a millimeter is about 1/25 of an inch.

In the metric system the kilometer is used instead of the mile. It equals about 5/8 of a mile.

Measurements of area are made by multiplying length by width, just as in the English system. The metric system unit of land area is 10 meters square and is called an *are* (pronounced AIR). The *hectare* is 100 meters square. Where the customary system uses square yards and square inches, the metric system uses square meters and square centimeters.

The *cubic meter* is used to measure volume, including the tonnage of ships or the contents of tanks and reservoirs. For smaller volumes of liquid there is the *milliliter*. The milliliter is a handy measure in chemistry, pharmacy, medicine, and other scientific work. The measurement "cc," used by doctors and chemists, is the abbreviation for cubic centimeter. But it also stands for a milliliter, which is exactly the same amount.

The *hectoliter* is used for the things we measure in bushels. It is nearly 3 bushels. Things we count by quarts or gallons are measured in liters.

The kilogram, which is a little more than 2 pounds, is used in everyday trade instead of the pound. A metric ton is 1,000 kilograms.

It's all very logical.

AVOIRDUPOIS
WEIGHT

Suppose you work in a lumberyard at a seaport. You know that lumber is measured in *board feet*. A board foot is 1 foot long, 1 foot wide, and 1 inch thick. Easy, right?

Then, one day you have to buy some hickory logs. But when you start to figure out the board feet you're baffled, because the logs are round. You have to learn a way of measuring round logs. You measure them by the *cord*. A cord is 4 feet wide, 4 feet high, and 8 feet long. (Logs were once measured with a cord.)

When you arrange to have the logs brought to your port by rail, you find out that now the logs are figured by the *hundredweight*. You pay their freight at so much per hundred pounds. And then, because the logs are going to be shipped abroad, you have to pay ocean freight, and you pay that by the ton.

Ship carrying 5,100,000 board feet
of fir, hemlock, and cedar

Now, suppose the logs have landed at a French port. You have to pay dock rent. By weight or by the cord? Neither. You pay by the amount of space the logs take up on the wharf. The person who ordered the logs comes to measure them. But he's French and uses the metric system, so he doesn't care about board feet or cords. He figures the amount of wood in cubic meters.

The logs are still just logs. Before they are made into something else, they will have been weighed or measured in dozens of different ways. The same thing happens to almost everything around you.

Wherever in the world people do business, they need ways to measure, weigh, or count the goods they are trading. The customary weight system that is generally used for everyday commerce in the United States is the avoirdupois system, mentioned earlier. The avoirdupois system of weights is used in all English-speaking countries, so their trading partners use it, too. It is used for weighing all commodities except precious stones, metals, and medicines.

The units of avoirdupois weight (and their abbreviations) are:

The GRAIN (gr)

The DRAM (dr)

The OUNCE (oz)

The POUND (lb)

The HUNDREDWEIGHT (cwt)

The TON (tn)

Ears of wheat

THE GRAIN

The grain is the smallest unit of the system. It was probably the first weight standard, and it has been used for thousands of years. The actual standard was originally a grain of wheat taken from the middle of the wheat ear. The grain is the basic unit of all systems of weight. Grains in all systems are alike. In the customary system, 7,000 grains weigh a pound.

THE DRAM

There are 27.3437 grains in a dram, a word taken from an old Greek word that meant "a handful." It seems odd to have a fraction of such a small thing as a grain, but here's how it happened.

In 1303 when Edward I of England established avoirdupois weight for use in commerce, he ruled that the avoirdupois pound would have 16 ounces instead of 12, as the troy pound had. But the pound itself did not change. When it was divided by 12, all the ounces, drams, and grains came out evenly. When it was divided by 16, there was part of a grain left over.

Edward's idea wasn't really new. The Greeks had used a 16-ounce pound along with a 12-ounce pound, just as we do today in avoirdupois and troy weight. The Romans used a 12-ounce pound; they divided most of their weights and measures into twelfths. The word *ounce* means "a twelfth part."

THE HUNDREDWEIGHT

A hundred pounds make a *hundredweight*. Queen Elizabeth I of England gave it a little extra measure by adding 12 pounds to it. This is called a *long hundredweight* and is common today. The hundredweight has other names. It may be called a central or a quintal.

TONS:
LONG, SHORT, AND OTHER KINDS

Nobody is quite sure how the measurement of a ton began. Some people say it started as a tun, a huge cask that was used to hold wine. Others say it started as a chaldron, a wheat measure that held about 32 bushels. However it began, we know that it first came into use in northern Europe.

Twenty hundredweight—2,000 pounds—make a ton, sometimes called a *short ton*. Another common ton weighs 2,240 pounds and is made of 20 long hundredweight. This heavier ton is called a *long ton*. Long tons are generally used in England, while short tons are most common in the United States, Canada, and Australia.

A *register ton* is a unit of volume used in shipping. It tells how much a ship holds and is equal to 100 cubic feet.

A *cargo ton* measures the space taken up by freight. It varies, depending on the cargo. It's the volume of the freight that weighs a ton.

The *displacement ton* is used to figure the displacement of a ship, which is the amount of water a ship displaces, or pushes out of the way. A displacement ton is equal to an amount of seawater weighing a long ton—about 35 cubic feet of seawater.

A *kip* is half a ton, or 1,000 pounds. The first two letters are from the word "kilo," and the "p" stands for pounds. A *quarter* is a quarter of a large measure, such as a ton or a hundredweight.

The word *last* originally meant a load of cargo. But today it refers to a number of things. A last is usually 2 tons, or 4,000 pounds, but the exact weight varies from country to country and for different commodities.

A last of grain is 8½ bushels in the United States, 80 bushels in England. A last of gunpowder is 24 barrels, each weighing 100 pounds. A last of herring is 10,000, 13,200, or 20,000 fish. A last of hides is 12 dozen. A last of wool is 12 sacks. A last of flax or feathers is 1,700 pounds.

CAPACITY

Capacity, the amount a container holds, is an important measurement. In the beginning, the measures of capacity were natural objects—gourds, big clamshells, even eggshells. But natural measures of capacity varied. There were large gourds and small gourds, big shells and small shells. So it became necessary for sellers and buyers to have standards of capacity.

The first standard of capacity was used in Babylon. It was a hollow cube, each side of which was a handbreadth long. This cube, filled with water, was the Babylonian unit of capacity.

Water is still used as a standard for measuring capacity. The weight of the cubeful of water became a standard unit of weight, too.

Most of our measures of capacity today are measures not only of the amount they hold but also of the weight of that amount. For instance, a bushel basket holds a certain amount of grain, and a bushel of grain, by law, has a definite weight.

BUSHELS AND BUSHELS

The *bushel* is a dry measure used for such things as grains, fruits, and vegetables. The bushel is the largest dry measure in the customary system. The *pint* is the smallest.

The bushel, as a measure, must have changed over time, because the word came from old Celtic and meant "the hollowed hand." (The Celts lived in the British Isles and northern Europe.) It would take quite a number of hollowed hands to make the bushel of today.

Bushels of apples

American and English standard bushels are not the same. The American standard bushel contains 32 dry quarts, while the English customary bushel holds 33.026 quarts. The American standard bushel is the same as the old British Winchester bushel that was used back in the days when Henry VIII was still a boy.

When America was first settled, the colonists, being mostly English, used the English weights and measures they were used to. After the United States became independent, those standards were so much a part of business that they were adopted without change. The United States still uses those original measures, but in the nineteenth century England revised some of its measures. That is why, even though we use the same system, there are differences in certain standards.

The U.S. Bureau of Standards sets standard bushel measurements, and trade between the states is based on that bushel. But in some states it is the custom to measure a bushel in *heaped measure*, which means that the contents are piled high in the basket. Other states use *struck measure*, where the contents are level with the top of the basket.

The weights of bushels of different commodities vary. A bushel of something light and bulky, like charcoal, weighs only 20 pounds, while a bushel of salt weighs 80 pounds. So the law fixes a definite weight for a bushel of each commodity, varying only where states use heaped or struck measures.

A special measure of about 8 bushels is called a *seam*. A seam was the amount that could be carried on a packsaddle, so it, too, varied with different commodities. A horse can carry different amounts of different things.

A *peck* is 1/4 of a bushel, 8 quarts dry measure. At one time a peck was a special-sized pot used for measuring grain.

A *quart* is 2 pints, 1/8 of a peck dry measure. In liquid measure it is 1/4 of a gallon. The word is short for "a quarter part."

A *pint* is 1/2 of a quart in both dry and liquid measure. It was originally a small measure for wine.

THE GALLON

The *gallon* has been a measure for so long that nobody seems to know where it began. (The name comes from an old Gallic word for "bowl.") Both American and British gallons contain 4 quarts, but the British Imperial gallon is 1/5 larger than the U.S. standard gallon. The American gallon is exactly the same as the old English wine gallon, which had 32 ounces to the quart. The British Imperial gallon has 40 ounces to the quart. Another British gallon, called the barn gallon, is 2½ times larger than the Imperial gallon and is usually used for measuring wine.

Redividing a unit is a matter of convenience. In gasoline pumps, for instance, gallons are divided into tenths because that's a handy way to figure the price.

SOMETHING ABOUT CONTAINERS

As ways of doing business changed, units changed, too. Today, there is machinery to lift huge loads. Freight can be packed into giant containers that are hoisted aboard ships and freight cars with cranes. When workers loaded cargo without machinery, the containers had to be smaller.

Things that must be handled partly by hand come in smaller containers today than they once did. In the old days laborers had to strain over huge casks and bags. Now, most food and produce are packed in containers that are easier to lift.

Changed life-styles resulted in changed container sizes, too. When families were large and houses had plenty of storage room, people bought flour and sugar in 100-pound barrels and potatoes and onions in 100-pound bags. Now, not only do people have less space in which to store so much food, they also have no reason to buy such large quantities. If there isn't a market right around the corner, there's a fast way of getting to one.

THE BAG

Many products are measured by the containers in which they are shipped. Often a container of a certain size is almost a standard for a certain product. But you can't depend on it!

Suppose you are shopping around for a bag of coffee. If you buy it in Brazil, it would weigh a little over 132 pounds net. Net means not counting the container.

If you go to Colombia or Costa Rica for your bag of coffee, it would weigh 140 pounds gross. Gross weight includes the weight of the container.

If you buy your coffee from a merchant in Mexico or Venezuela, a bag would weigh 145 pounds gross. And if you decide to buy it in Guatemala you would have 160 pounds gross.

So you can see that when the word *bag* is used as a measurement, all you really know is that you have a closed paper, plastic, or fabric container. You would have to find out how big the bag was, what was in it, and where it came from before you would know how much it held. Sugar, wool, cement, and cocoa are all sold by the bag, and none of those bag weights is the same. You couldn't even depend on a simple bag of flour. The English sometimes pack their flour in bags that weigh six times as much as bags of flour in the United States.

The size of the bags in which produce is packed changes with the times, too. When food is scarce and expensive it is packed in smaller quantities.

A *sack* is not a fixed measure in the United States, but it is usually about 3 bushels. A sack of flour is 100 pounds if it is going to be sold in the United States and 140 if it is going to be exported. A sack of cotton is 140 pounds. A sack of salt is 315 pounds.

BARRELS AND BASKETS

The *barrel* is another container that is both a weight and a measure. Barrels of different things are measured in different ways. A barrel of beef, pork, or fish is measured by weight. Its standard is 200 pounds.

A barrel of flour weighs only 196 pounds, but because this weight has been used for so many hundreds of years nobody changes it. Flour was first weighed against one of the oldest weights we know, the stone. Long ago, goods really were weighed against stones instead of metal. One particular size of stone weighed about 14 pounds. That weight is still used today and is called a *stone*. For hundreds of years a barrel of flour has weighed 14 stones, or 196 pounds.

Packing tobacco in barrels in colonial Virginia

Barrels of fruits and vegetables are measured by inches instead of by weight. A fruit or vegetable barrel must hold 7,056 cubic inches of produce.

A barrel of liquids is measured by gallons. Once it held a little more than 31 gallons, but now, so they will be easier to lift and handle, 15-gallon barrels are usual.

Oil is usually shipped in a special metal barrel called a *drum*, which holds from 50 to 55 gallons.

A *hogshead* is a very large barrel or cask. Nobody seems to know where the hogshead got its name. In different places, a hogshead might hold any amount from 63 to 140 gallons. A hogshead that holds 126 is called a *pipe*.

Another kind of large cask, used to ship wine, is called a *butt*. A butt holds 130 standard gallons. The Greeks were the first to use the butt. From that word came the name of one of our most common containers—the bottle.

The amounts held by different kinds of trade baskets are set by law.

Bunches of grapes are packed in *climax baskets*, the long baskets with handles and solid bottoms. Climax baskets may hold anything from a half-pint dry measure to several quarts. Round stave baskets, the big ones that apples are sold in, are *bushel baskets*. And when you buy a *splint basket* of strawberries, you are getting a pint or a quart.

COUNTING

In doing business, many things are counted instead of being weighed or measured. The most common way of counting is by the dozen, which is 12.

The Romans did most of their business in dozens. It was a natural part of their duodecimal system. (*Duo* means "two" and *decem* means "ten," in Latin, the Roman language.)

A dozen is handy for buying eggs or rolls, but if you are buying things in quantity you would buy them by the *gross*, which is 12 dozen, or by the *great gross*, which is 12 gross.

A *score* is a way of counting that isn't much used in business. A score is 20. When Lincoln said, "Fourscore and seven years ago," he meant 87 years.

———— SOME FUNNY MEASURES ————

A *catty* is an old Chinese unit of weight for rice. The amount grew smaller between the rice field and the market because the laborers who carried the rice bags ate some on the way. When they reached the market, the rice bags weighed less than they did when they started out, but they still measured the same number of catties. The rice that was eaten didn't count.

A *hand* is a measure of bananas. It's one of the small bunches that grows on the big bunch. People in the banana business call the whole big bunch a *stem*. Each banana is called a *finger*.

A *cran* is a measurement used only for fresh herring. A cran of herring is 45 gallons. The Gauls, people who lived in western Europe two thousand years ago, first used the word as a measure. The word meant "a lot." A cran is certainly a lot of herring.

A *firkin* is a British weight for butter—56 pounds of it. Sometimes, though, a firkin is 9 gallons or 1/4 of a barrel.

A *frail* is 50 pounds of raisins. Originally it was a rush basket that was used in Mediterranean countries for figs and raisins. The basket isn't used anymore, but the amount it held is still called by that name.

A *clove* is a British measurement for cheese or wool—8 or 10 pounds of either one.

A *ship pound* isn't a pound at all but a unit of weight varying between 300 and 400 pounds.

At one time a *barge* must have been the load

carried by a barge of a certain size, because a barge of freight weighs 21.2 long tons.

A *baker's dozen* isn't 12—it's 13. This started in England, during the time of Oliver Cromwell, when bakers were ordered to make their rolls smaller to save flour. Customers were angry at getting less for their money, so to keep their good will, bakers threw an extra roll into every dozen.

TROY WEIGHT: —MONEY, JEWELS,— AND PRECIOUS METALS

Before people used money, they had to trade. If you had an extra ox and you needed a sword, you tried to trade the ox for the sword. There was no such thing as "change." Your ox might be worth more than the sword, but you couldn't get a sword and a half for the ox. You couldn't give three-quarters of an ox, either. The only thing you might do would be to persuade the other person to throw in a belt or a pair of sandals to even things up a bit.

Where people kept oxen and cows, these animals were the earliest measures of wealth. Even when gold first came into use, its value was reckoned by how many oxen or cows an amount of gold was worth. (Later, when coins were made, some of the early ones were just rough copper bars stamped with a picture of an ox.) Today we think in exactly the opposite way. We think of how much gold a cow is worth. But in those very early days cows were money. You could exchange them for anything you needed, even if you couldn't take them to market in your pocket.

Sometime in the late Stone Age, the Egyptians got the idea that gold, which they knew was rare and therefore valuable, could be exchanged for other things. At first, they didn't know how to mine gold. They obtained their earliest supplies by chasing the Nubians and taking away their gold beads and ornaments.

Of course, they couldn't get much gold that way so they ground the gold ornaments into gold dust and used small amounts of that to exchange for goods. The Egyptians measured this gold dust by the amount a goose quill would hold. Then they invented a way to weigh it, using a primitive balance scale with plant seeds weighed against the gold. This use of seeds as weights has come down to us over thousands of years. We still use the grain, which is a seed, as a weight for gold. We also use the *carat* for weighing gold and precious stones. The carat was first measured by a bean weighing 4 grains. Now its standard is 3.086 grains. Sometimes you see carat spelled with a k. That very small bean was called a karob.

Once they started mining gold, the Egyptians measured large amounts by the *heket,* a common measure something like our bushel. Then they discovered something interesting. Two hekets of gold were not always equally heavy, even though they were the same size. They found that the gold in their mines was sometimes naturally fused with silver. Since silver is much lighter than gold, this gold and silver mixture was not as heavy as pure gold. So the only way the Egyptians had for testing the purity of their gold and determining its value was by weighing it against a standard weight they called a *beqa*. The beqa was a small stone cylinder with domed ends that equalled a weight of pure gold. These weights for gold were the ancestors of all the weights in the world, and the gold beads that the Egyptians stole from the Nubians were the beginning of money.

The special system used for weighing precious metal is called *troy weight*. Some people think that this system started in the town of Troyes in France, but nobody is really sure. By the fourteenth century troy weight was being used extensively in England. The English kings used it to count the royal treasure, and in 1527 it became the legal standard for minting coins. But it was in common use long before that. In 1266 Henry III had said, "An English penny, called a sterling, round and without any clippings, shall weigh 32 wheatcorns in the middle of the ear. Twenty pence do make an ounce, and 12 ounces a pound."

We use some troy weight measurements today. The units of troy weight are:

The GRAIN (gr)
The PENNYWEIGHT (dwt)
The OUNCE (oz t)
The POUND (lb t)

THE GRAIN
AND
THE PENNYWEIGHT

The *grain* is the smallest unit of troy weight, as it is in avoirdupois weight. But there are only 5,760 grains in a troy pound. There are 7,000 grains in an avoirdupois pound.

Twenty-four grains make a *pennyweight*, which was the weight of the English penny when troy weight became the legal standard.

THE OUNCE
AND
THE POUND

Twenty pennyweights, or 480 grains, make a *troy ounce*. We said that the word "ounce" originally meant a twelfth part. An ounce was a twelfth of a Roman pound and of Henry III's pound. Twelve ounces make a pound in troy weight.

Troy weight is the basic system, but money-minters and jewelers also use other weights.

The *barleycorn* is another word for the grain. Sometimes a grain of barley was used instead of a grain of wheat. The weight is the same—1/24 of a pennyweight.

The carat is the unit of weight for precious stones as well as for gold. A carat is usually divided into four parts for handier measuring, and each part is called a *carat grain*. If a jewel weighs more than an even number of carats, jewelers say, "a carat and an eighth" or "two and 1/32 carats."

**World's largest black diamond,
the 42-carat 'Rembrandt' diamond,
shown next to an average-sized
1.3 carat stone**

Grading precious stones by carats is a long and tedious job; this is how Cecil Rhodes once kept control of the diamond market. Cecil Rhodes was an Englishman who went to Africa in 1870 and began mining for diamonds. Because he eventually came to own the largest diamond mines in the world, he was able to control the price of diamonds everywhere. The owners of a number of other diamond mines got together and decided to break his power by pooling all their diamonds and putting a great number of them on the market at once. They called Rhodes in and showed him the diamonds, all carefully graded, set out on a long table. As he rose to leave, Rhodes bumped into the table and knocked it over, scattering the diamonds in every direction. It took years to sort and grade the diamonds again, and by that time it was too late for the scheme to work.

A carat is also used to measure the purity of gold. For the sake of convenience, pure gold is divided into 24 parts, each part called a carat. This measurement is then used to show how much gold is used in a mixture with other metals. Something marked 14-carat gold (or 14K) means that 14 parts of gold are mixed with 10 parts of another metal. Twenty-two-carat gold is almost pure gold, with 2 carats of another metal added just to harden it. (Pure gold is very soft.) Measuring the purity of gold was what the Egyptians were after when they first started weighing gold.

The minter, who coins money, uses the *mite*, which is 1/20 of a grain. Thousands of years ago it was the name of a coin of very small value. The Bible talks about the "widow's mite."

Sterling is the measurement of the purity of silver. Once it meant that the silver was 0.925 pure. Now the standard for sterling is 0.50 silver.

ABOUT MONEY

For a long time precious metal was simply something to trade. People might trade gold for a cow, then trade the cow for cloth or jewels. They didn't have one common thing that they could exchange for anything else they wanted, the way we use money today.

People finally got around to using precious metals as a medium of exchange for other things, but they always exchanged an equal value of metal for whatever they were buying with it. That's not what we do today.

The ancient Greeks were the first to use coins with the value they represented stamped on the face of the coin. After that it wasn't necessary to weigh gold or silver every time you made a business deal because the coin's value was written right on it. And each coin actually contained its face value in precious metal. To prevent this metal from being pared away, money-minters began milling the edges of the coins—making those little ridges we still have around the edges of our gold and silver coins. Coins that were worth large amounts were made of pure gold. Coins of smaller value were of silver and no bigger than your smallest fingernail.

Ancient Greek coins

American $30 paper bill (1776)

Nowadays, metal money isn't actually worth the amount stamped on the coin. The money used in each country can be exchanged for a reasonable amount of goods only when that money is backed up by things of real value.

Every country in the world has its own units of money, regulated by law. The law says how much precious metal must go into each coin and how much gold, property, or other treasure must back up every paper note. Of course, paper money has no value by itself. It is worthless unless it represents things of real value that are too bulky or impossible to trade.

When there is inflation, money doesn't buy very much. Sometimes that's because there is more money than there are things to buy with it. When this happens, prices get very high. Sometimes there is inflation because a government has printed money that isn't backed by any real treasure and the people know it. Whatever the reason, the less you can get in exchange for your money, the less it is worth—no matter what is printed on it. Money today, like money 5,000 years ago, is good only when it can be traded for real things.

In the United States the dollar is the main unit of money. The American dollar started as the Spanish peso when Florida and the West Indies were settled by the Spanish. The peso was worth 8 Spanish reals, smaller coins each worth about 12½ cents. That's why the pirates who sailed the Spanish Main (we call it the Caribbean Sea now) called dollars "pieces of eight."

The slang word for a Spanish real was a "bit." When there weren't any bits around, people cut their silver dollars into four parts, which made each part worth two reals, or two bits. We still use that slang today. A quarter of a dollar is two bits, a half dollar is four bits, and 75 cents is six bits.

The first U.S. silver dollar was minted in 1794 and was modeled after the Spanish peso. It was called the "pillar dollar" because it had two pillars embossed on it with a ribbon twined around them. That was the beginning of the dollar sign ($). There was a reason for using the peso as the model for the dollar. During the Revolutionary War the Continental Congress had promised to pay all obligations in pesos—Spanish silver dollars.

Until 1873 the silver dollar was the legal monetary unit in the United States. In 1879 the gold standard law was passed, saying that all government bonds and paper bills over $20 could be exchanged for gold. In 1933 President Franklin D. Roosevelt repealed the gold standard law.

The silver dollar we have now doesn't contain a dollar's worth of silver. The half dollar, the quarter, and the dime (which means a tenth) are all portions of the dollar, as their names show. They don't have much silver in them.

The metal in the nickel and the penny isn't worth much of anything. Because of this there is a law that says you can refuse to accept more than a quarter's worth of nickels or pennies in payment for anything. But people know that the government stands behind the value written on those coins so they hardly ever refuse to accept them.

When people stop believing in the money of a country they stop using it and go back to the old system of trading. They may exchange a baby carriage for a bicycle or a sweater for a pair of shoes. Sometimes something that everybody wants becomes a form of money that can be exchanged for anything else, the way cows were in the beginning. Coffee or stockings or anything at all that is scarce and in demand may be used for money. People are exchanging real things for real things, even if they are not actually of equal value. When nobody believes in the money of a country, a bushel basket of it might not be enough to buy a candy bar.

APOTHECARIES' ——WEIGHT AND—— SOME MEDICAL MEASUREMENTS

Until 1617 in England you could buy drugs and medicines not only from apothecaries but from grocers, too. They all mixed prescriptions in any way they thought best, using widely varying quantities and strengths of drugs.

But in 1617 the apothecaries (we call them pharmacists now) got a separate charter from the king, and after that no grocer was allowed to keep an apothecary shop. Physicians tried to get all apothecaries to fill prescriptions in the same way, but there were no generally accepted formulas in use.

In 1618 the doctors made up a recipe book, the *Pharmacopoeia*, for making prescriptions. They sent special agents to examine the apothecary shops. The agents had the power to destroy any compounds they found that had not been prepared according to the recipes in the *Pharmacopoeia*.

Today the *Pharmacopoeia*, always kept up-to-date, is still the legal standard for drugs and chemicals. Most countries publish their own, but early in the twentieth century an international conference at Brussels, Belgium, set up international standards for many basic drugs used in medicine. Now the United Nations has an agency whose job it is to agree on international standards to be used in different national pharmacopoeias.

Before 1825 physicians and apothecaries in England used an old system of weights and measures that was based on troy weight and the old wine gallon. Then laws were passed that set up standard weights and measures to be used in preparing medicines. Now, in addition to the apothecary system, pharmacists use the metric system and occasionally troy and avoirdupois weights.

Apothecaries' weights are usually indicated by symbols and Roman numerals instead of regular abbreviations. (That's one reason a doctor's prescription is hard to read, if you don't know the code.)

The basic unit of apothecaries' weight is the same as that of other systems, the grain.

Twenty grains make one *scruple*. A scruple was originally a small pointed stone used as a weight for tiny quantities. The sign for a scruple looks like this ℈ and a half scruple looks like this ℈ss.

Three scruples, or 60 grains, make a *drachm* or *dram*. (Remember that word, dram?) The Greeks called it a drachma, or handful. In old apothecary books the word *drams* is written *drachmae*, just as it was when this way of measuring began. The symbol for a dram in apothecaries' weight is ℨ.

Eight drams is 1 ounce apothecary, ℥.

Twelve apothecary ounces equal 1 *pound*, as in troy weight. An apothecary pound is written ℔.

Apothecaries often use liquid measures in making up prescriptions. The smallest liquid measure is a *minim*, which is just about one drop. It is written ♏.

Sixty minims make one *fluid dram*. Your doctor writes f℥.

Eight fluid drams make a *fluid ounce*, or f℥.

Four fluid ounces make a *gill*, a very old measure that isn't used much anymore. In many places, pharmacists now use the metric system.

SOME MEDICAL MEASUREMENTS

There are a number of measurements that help your doctor know how you are. Ever since the sixteenth and seventeenth centuries, when scientists began to find out how the human body really worked, they have tried to figure out ways of measuring how well, or how badly, it was functioning.

Your pulse rate tells the number of times your heart beats every minute, usually from 70 to 75 beats. When you are sick, excited, or frightened, it may beat much faster. Babies have a very fast heartbeat. As people get older, their heartbeat usually gets slower.

Birds and other small animals have very fast heartbeats. Large animals have very slow ones. If you took a horse's pulse you would find that its heart beats only from 28 to 40 times a minute.

As soon as doctors learned, early on, that they could count heartbeats by taking a pulse, they did it. They didn't need any instruments—only four fingers across the patient's wrist.

Doctors also knew, from early times, that sick people run a fever. Their body temperatures rise. You can feel a fever by putting a hand on someone's forehead—it feels hot. But your hand doesn't tell you how hot. You need a thermometer for that. If the thermometer is a glass rod with mercury in a bulb at the bottom, the mercury rises in the rod to register the degree of your temperature. Some new disposable thermometers are made of paper, with a chemical scale.

Normal body temperature is 98.6°F. When you are sick, it goes higher or lower.

Fish and reptiles do not have an internally regulated temperature. Their bodies take on the temperature of their surroundings. We call them cold-blooded animals.

Doctors also measure your blood pressure. This is the amount of pressure your heart puts on the walls of your arteries, which are the vessels that carry blood away from your heart to other parts of your body. The doctor's instrument measures blood pressure in millimeters of mercury. Normal blood pressure is from 100 to 140 millimeters.

You have two kinds of cells in your blood, red and white. The white ones fight disease or infection. A normal blood count is one white cell to more than six hundred red cells in a particular volume of blood. If you are sick, the white ones multiply fast to attack the problem. Your blood count shows more white cells than usual.

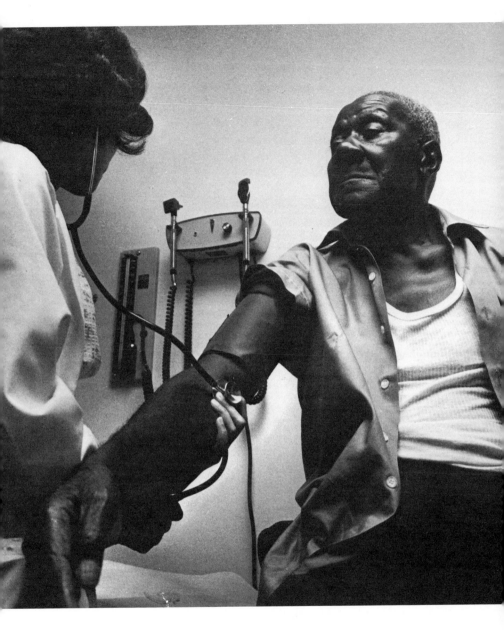

A nurse reading a patient's blood pressure

Today, a chemical analysis of just a small amount of blood can show a great many different things about how your body is working. Not too long ago doctors needed a number of instruments to measure those things.

DOING BUSINESS:
—————BUILDING—————

Architects, engineers, and builders need to measure all kinds of things, from bricks to air pressure to steel to the force of the wind.

One of the most important jobs in architectural engineering is the calculation of stresses and strains. How much strain will be put on any part of a structure? How strong must that part be to resist that strain? Buildings are also braced to resist the pressure of the wind. All big buildings are constructed to sway a little with the wind, because if they were completely rigid, they would break. Very high buildings sway as much as 3 feet. (A sign hanging in one of the top floor offices of the Empire State Building in New York reads, "Please keep your seat when the building is in motion.")

Before very high buildings are constructed, models are tested in a wind tunnel at the National Bureau of Standards. Another machine, a huge

press three stories tall, crushes walls to see how much weight they will hold.

Tensile strength refers to the greatest amount of strain any material can bear without breaking. It is usually figured by the number of pounds of pressure—called *newtons*— per square inch or square meter that are necessary to make a material tear or break. Before they are used, all kinds of materials are tested for tensile strength. Steel for buildings is tested. So is paper. So are silk and nylon, whether they are going to be used for stockings or parachutes. Even cookie manufacturers test the tensile strength of their cookies. If the cookie breaks easily, the dough is too thin. If it takes a lot of force to break the cookie, watch out for your digestion!

Air presses on a building. The upper floors press on the floors below, and the whole structure presses on the foundation. The measurement of this pressure on every square foot of the building is called *square foot pressure.* Buildings are designed to withstand this pressure.

The pressure on the floor area is created by what are called *dead load* and *live load.* Dead load is what the floor itself weighs plus the building weight it must hold. Live load is furniture, machinery, people, and the force of any movement on the floor.

Dead load and live load are figured differently for different kinds of buildings. A factory that is

Building a skyscraper in New York City

going to hold heavy industrial machinery must have a floor that will support 300 pounds for every square foot of floor area. A factory where the machinery is lighter will need a floor that can support 150 pounds for every square foot. The live load for theaters, meeting halls, stores, and showrooms is about 100 pounds per square foot. For an ordinary house it is only 60 pounds.

Once, houses were allowed to be converted into factories without any changes, and sometimes the floor collapsed, taking people, machinery, and the building with it. Now, the rules covering dead load and live load are very strict. The law requires everything to be made even stronger than it needs to be.

When figuring the load a roof will bear, not only the weight of the roof is counted but also the weight of rain and snow.

──────── BUILDING MATERIALS ────────

We said earlier that the unit of measurement for lumber was a board foot—a length of board 1 foot long, 1 foot wide, and 1 inch thick.

If you want to find the number of board feet in a board 3 inches thick, 4 inches wide, and 14 feet long, you would make the measurements into a fraction, like this:

$$\frac{3 \times 4 \times 14}{12}$$

The thickness and width of 3 inches by 4 inches would cancel the 12 inches (1 foot), so you would see that you had 14 board feet in the plank. You pay for lumber by the board foot.

Another measure for lumber, used for fancy moldings and narrow strips of wood, is called a *running foot*. Only the length of the wood is measured.

Steel is measured by the ton.

Bricks are measured by the thousand. Figuring how many bricks will be needed for a job is called *estimating*. An experienced mason (bricklayer) can estimate very close to the actual number of bricks required.

Cement is measured by the bag or the barrel. A bag of cement weighs 94 pounds net. A barrel of cement is 4 bags, weighing 376 pounds.

Lime comes by the barrel, too—either 180 or 280 pounds.

Pipe is measured in inches.

The thickness of wire is measured in thousandths of an inch. A thousandth of an inch is called a *mil*.

Nails come by the keg. A keg of nails is 100 pounds.

A nail may seem like a small thing, but there is a lot to measuring a nail. The system for describing the length of the most commonly used nails is called the *penny system*, which began in England and is so old that nobody remembers exactly how it started. Six-penny nails are 6 inches long. Two-penny nails are 2 inches long. Some people think that at one time a hundred 6-inch nails cost sixpence and maybe the short, 2-inch nails cost twopence.

Nail lengths are written 2d, 3d, etc., up to 60d. (The d is from the name of an old Roman coin, the *denier*. Now d stands for a penny.)

Wallpaper comes by the roll. There are 30 square feet in a single roll of wallpaper, so the length of the roll depends on its width. Narrow rolls are usually 8 yards long and wider ones are 5 yards. There are also double rolls and triple rolls. French wallpapers usually come in double rolls, and English wallpaper is usually 1½ times as long as a single roll. To estimate how much wallpaper you will need for a room, you measure the number of square feet of wall surface, subtract the area of doors and windows, and divide by 30.

DOING BUSINESS:
—WHAT WE WEAR—

The business of making clothing is very old. So are the measurements that are used.

THE RAW MATERIALS

Wool, cotton, flax, leather, and silk have all been used to make clothes for thousands of years, so traders had to find ways to package and sell them. Putting them in bags was one way. Of all the bag measurements, a bag of wool is the biggest. It weighs 364 pounds.

The English have another bag of wool that weighs 182 pounds. They call it a *pocket*. The pockets we have in our clothes today began as enormous bags and pouches for carrying merchandise. Gradually pockets shrank until they were small enough to be carried by hand or attached to a belt. And finally, they were sewed right into the clothes.

Scene of plantation life in the American South, showing baling of cotton

A *sack* is different from a bag. A sack of cotton weighs 140 pounds in the United States and twice as much in England.

But usually, cotton is measured by the *bale*. Baling raw materials is an old way to pack them. You simply tie the goods into big, tight bundles for shipping or storing. Many kinds of things, from cotton and rags to hay, are baled.

Every country that grows cotton bales it, and each country has its own bale weight. A bale of cotton from the United States weighs 500 pounds, from Egypt 740, from India 400, and from Brazil or Peru 250 pounds.

Sometimes cotton yarn is measured by the *block*. A block is a few *hanks*, which are big coils of yarn, tied into a small bale of about 5 pounds. A *sarpler* is a bale of wool that weighs a long ton, 2,240 pounds.

--------------------- YARN ---------------------

Raw materials spun into yarn or thread have another set of measurements all their own. *Denier* (deh-NEAR) is one of the most important.

Denier is the measure of weight for all silk and synthetic yarns. When Francis I started the modern silk industry in sixteenth-century France, he looked for a weight to use for silk thread. He finally decided on an old silver Roman coin about the size of a fingernail. The coin was called a denier.

A thread of 1-denier size would measure about 4.5 million yards to a pound. As the denier size gets larger, the number of yards in a pound gets smaller. The higher the denier size, the thicker the yarn.

In the textile industry there is a relationship between the length of yarn and its weight. The English yard and pound are the standards for measuring spun yarns all over the world. They are numbered according to how many yards there are to the pound. This count is expressed in deniers.

A *typp* (pronounced "tip") is a unit used for all yarns. It refers to the number of thousands of yards of a particular yarn that weigh one pound. The word comes from using the initial letters of the words *thousand yards per pound.*

Often, yarn is formed into a sort of knot called a *skein.* Skeins of different materials have different lengths, but a skein of cotton yarn is always 360 feet. A very large skein is called a *hank.* There are 840 yards of cotton yarn in a hank and 560 yards of woolen yarn.

As yarn is spun, it is wound onto a rod called a *spindle,* and this is used as a measure, too, because it holds a certain amount of each kind of yarn. There are 15,120 yards of cotton yarn on a spindle and 14,400 yards of linen yarn.

Here are some other measurements for yarn:

A thread of cotton is 1½ yards.

A *lea* of silk or cotton thread is 120 yards. A lea of linen is 300 yards.

A *heer* is a measure so old that nobody knows where it came from. It is 600 yards of wool or linen yarn.

MEASURING CLOTH

In the United States, the yard is the standard for the textile industry, and it measures 36 inches. For making finished clothes there are other ways of measuring cloth. A yardstick is 36 inches long. There are special curved yardsticks for measuring pattern pieces where curved lines are used, such as sleeve caps. Tape measures are used, too. Most tape measures are 60 inches long.

An old measure of cloth that was used before the yard was the *ell*, which might be anywhere from 24 to 48 inches. In places where the ell is still used, it is the length of a meter. The ell has been used as a measure since biblical times. It was first measured from the hand, around the elbow, and back to the hand again, which was certainly a convenient way to estimate the length of goods. In the tenth century King Edgar of England standardized the ell at 36 inches, which became a yard.

The material in a bolt of cloth is so tightly rolled that it looks like a long, flat club. A bolt of cotton is about 40 yards, wool about 70. Depending on the materials, bolts of goods have different widths. Silk, cotton, or synthetic dress goods are usually either 30 inches, a yard, or 45 inches wide. Woolens are 60 inches wide and upholstery materials are woven in 54-inch widths.

Sometimes a piece of cloth of a new design is run off to test the pattern for effect and to see how it looks made into a dress or a coat. This is called a *book* or *run of goods*. To allow plenty of material for experimenting, a book is usually about 50 yards. A *cut of goods* is about 5 yards, enough to make an average dress.

CLOTH INTO CLOTHES: SIZES

Pattern sizes for suits or dresses are not exact measurements. Each manufacturer has his or her own patterns. One manufacturer's dress size 12 may have a waistline an inch or two smaller than another's, or the dress may be wider or bigger in the shoulders. Manufacturers change their patterns as styles change.

Patterns for dresses that are made for "juniors" are very different from patterns made for older women because junior body shapes are different. Junior sizes run 5, 7, 9, 11, and so on. Regular sizes have even numbers—8, 10, 12, 14, and so on. Some patterns for larger figures are made in half sizes, and patterns for short women are called "petites."

When a new pattern is created from a design, a standard pattern is made first. Then larger and smaller sizes are figured from that standard. This is called *grading.*

The sizes of most men's clothes are measured in inches—inches around the neck, waist, chest, and the length of arms and legs. Where it's important, two or more sizes are given. Shirt size, for example, has the number of inches around the neck plus the length, in inches, of the sleeves.

Trimmings have their own measurements. The size of a button is measured by its diameter—the width across the middle of the button. The unit of measurement is called a *line,* and it is 1/40 of an inch. So a 16-line button would be 16 times 1/40, or 2/5 of an inch wide.

SHOES

Shoe patterns are wooden forms called *lasts,* and like dress patterns, the lasts of different companies are different. That's why you may be comfortable in the shoes of one manufacturer while the same size shoe from another makes your feet hurt. Even if the size is right, the shape of the shoe might not be right for the shape of your foot.

If your foot is measured for a pair of shoes, you step on a ruler that is measured off in inches, by eighths of an inch. If you look at the ruler you will see that your shoe size is not equal to the number of inches in the length of your foot. The place where you put your heel has no numbers. The measurement starts underneath the arch of your foot. So if you wear a size 6, the distance from your arch to the end of your big toe is 6 inches.

The width of your foot is important, too. Foot widths run from A to E. An EE is a wide foot, and for very narrow feet there are double A's, triple A's, all the way to AAAA.

The thickness of shoe leather is measured in ounces. A shoemaking ounce is 1/64 of an inch. For measuring the thickness of the material that is going to be the sole, units called *irons* are used. An iron is 1/48 of an inch.

In some places, shoemakers still use a barley-corn as a measure of length. It is 1/3 of an inch, the size of a grain of barley.

English sizes are almost the same as those in the United States, but other European sizes are completely different. A size 8 shoe in the United States is a 24 in many European countries. Clothes sizes on the European continent are very different, too. Gloves are measured by the number of inches around your hand and your fingers when you make a fist.

HATS

Women's hat sizes are simple. They are the measurement in inches around the head. If you wear a size 22 hat, your head is 22 inches around.

Men's hat sizes are more complicated, but they are also based on the number of inches around the head. Here is how it is supposed to work: You take a tape measure and measure the distance around your head. Then you lay the tape measure down in a circle, just as it came off your head. The diameter—the distance across the center of the circle—would be your hat size. If the circle is 22 inches around, the diameter is 7 and that's your size.

Actually, in the United States, it doesn't work quite that way. The diameter of the circle on which hat sizes are based is 5/32 of an inch smaller than it should be. That's because back in the early days the man who made most of the shapes on which hats were blocked couldn't figure very well. His basic form was 5/32 of an inch off, but so many hats were made on it that people got used to that size and never bothered to change it.

COOKING
——MEASUREMENTS——

Cooking measurements are ordinary dry and liquid measures, whether the cook is preparing food for one person at home or for a restaurant full of people. But even if you don't have some of the standard measures handy, you can get by if you know what equals what.

2 cups of liquid = 1 pint
4 cups = 1 quart
1 pint of liquid = 1 pound (Most liquids weigh about the same, except the thick, syrupy ones such as molasses.)
2 cups of granulated sugar = 1 pound
2½ cups of confectioner's sugar = 1 pound
2⅔ cups of brown sugar = 1 pound
4 cups of flour = 1 pound
2 cups of butter = 1 pound
1/4 pound of butter = 1/2 cup

12 tablespoons of flour or sugar = 1 cup
2 tablespoons of butter or sugar = 1 ounce
4 tablespoons of flour = 1 ounce
2 tablespoons of liquid = 1 ounce
1 tablespoon of salt = 1 ounce
60 drops of a liquid such as water = 1 teaspoon
3 teaspoons = 1 tablespoon
16 tablespoons = 1 cup

Here are some measurements cooks have always used:

a handful is about 3/4 cup
a coffee cup is about 3/4 cup
a wine glass is about 1/4 cup
a small teacup is about 1/2 cup
a salt spoon is about 1/4 tsp
a quill is a roll of dried cinnamon
a gyle is one brewing of beer or ale
and a temperature between 250 and 266°F is called
   candy height.

Measurements in cooking are supposed to be absolutely level. But some cooks use a handful of this and a pinch of that and make wonderful things to eat.

SCIENCE IS
—— MEASUREMENT ——

Until something can be measured in some way, it cannot be completely understood. Before people could measure the size of the earth and the other planets, the distances between the planets and the sun, and the size of the sun itself, we didn't really understand the solar system. Until there was a way to measure the distances to other galaxies and the speed with which objects are traveling in space, we couldn't begin to understand the universe. Every advance in ways of measuring means that we understand a little more about the universe we live in.

Scientists today can measure the mass of the sun, which is 93 million miles away, and the mass of an electron, which is millions of times too small to see. They know the temperatures of stars (by their color) and how fast light travels. As scientists pursue knowledge, they discover or invent new and better ways of measuring things that have never been measured before.

A hundred and fifty years ago people thought their ways of measuring were precise. They were building railroads, steamships, dams, and machinery that needed exactness to 1/100 of an inch. Now scientists measure in the millionths of an inch. They weigh things that have practically no mass and measure the speed of fast-moving invisible particles.

Ordinary standards of length, mass, and volume don't begin to meet the needs of science today. Electricity, light, heat, time, and many other things that can't be held or weighed, seen or touched, need to be measured, too. Scientists have had to invent standard units for measuring them.

MEASURING ENERGY

Energy is the ability to do work. Over the centuries people have learned how to harness many kinds of energy, or the forces in nature that generate energy. Measuring those forces aids in putting them to work.

Forces either make things move or prevent them from moving. It takes energy to start or to stop a moving object.

A *foot-pound* is a unit of energy. It's the energy needed to raise a weight of 1 pound to a height of 1 foot in one second. (In the metric system a similar force is called a *Newton-meter* or *joule*, pronounced "jowl.")

Manpower is another measurement of energy.

An average man can lift a weight of 90 pounds 1 foot in 1 second. This is called 1 manpower.

Horsepower is a bigger unit of energy. By running a great many tests, the inventor James Watt figured out that an average horse could lift a weight of 550 pounds 1 foot off the ground in 1 second. So it was agreed that an engine with the same power would be a 1-horsepower engine. A 100-horsepower engine has the power of 100 horses.

MEASURING HEAT

Heat is energy. A unit of heat, measured on a particular scale, is called a *degree*. The constant rate at which mercury expands in a thermometer measures degrees of heat. Whether the thermometer is in your mouth measuring your body temperature or outside the house measuring air temperature, the mercury in the thermometer expands and rises, or contracts and falls, as the temperature around it changes.

The two most commonly used thermometer scales are Fahrenheit and Celsius (also called centigrade). The Fahrenheit scale was devised by Gabriel Fahrenheit, a German physicist who introduced the use of mercury in thermometers. On the Fahrenheit scale the freezing point is 32° above zero. Water freezes at that temperature. On this scale, water boils at 212° above zero.

Celsius is a metric scale. It was devised by Anders Celsius, a Swedish astronomer, in the eighteenth century. Centigrade, the former name for Celsius, means "a hundred steps." On the Celsius thermometer scale, water freezes at 0° and boils at 100°. Nobody has ever made anything cold enough to measure the lowest limit of coldness, which is called *absolute zero,* but scientists have come close enough to figure it at −273°C (−459°F). No one has been able to estimate the upper limit of hotness, either. The center of the sun is thought to be about 40,000,000°C.

To change degrees Celsius to degrees Fahrenheit, multiply the Celsius temperature by 9/5 and add 32. To change from Fahrenheit to Celsius, subtract 32 from the Fahrenheit temperature and multiply what you have left by 5/9.

Kelvin is a measurement of temperature based on color. Color, which is a form of light, is also a form of heat. If you've ever seen a piece of very hot metal, you know how color, light, and heat are related. As the metal gets hotter, it glows red. When it gets hotter still it glows white. Kelvin temperature changes with color.

On the Kelvin thermometer scale, zero is at −273° Celsius, or −459.4° Fahrenheit. The temperature of sunlight in the middle of the day is about 6,000° Kelvin.

The amount of heat necessary to raise the temperature of 1 gram of water 1 degree Celsius is called a *calorie.* (The word *calorie* was taken from the Latin word for heat.) One calorie is a very small amount, so scientists invented another unit of 1,000 calories. What's confusing is that the word *calorie* is used for both sizes. Scientists often call the larger one a kilocalorie.

The food you eat releases energy. When you talk about calories in food, you are actually talking about kilocalories.

———————— **MEASURING ELECTRICITY** ————————

Electricity is a kind of energy. An *ampere* is the measurement of the flow of electric current. Amperes were named after the French scientist André Ampere, who was the first to invent a way to measure electricity.

Just as a certain number of gallons of water will flow through a pipe in a certain amount of time, a definite number of amperes will flow through a wire. When electric current pushes through a wire, other electrical particles in that wire work to keep it from flowing. This pushing against the current is called resistance, and it is measured in *ohms*. Ohms were named after George S. Ohm, the German scientist who discovered the way resistance works in an electric circuit.

A *volt* is the measurement of the amount of electromotive force needed to drive 1 ampere of current through a resistance of 1 ohm. Volts push amperes through a wire. The volt was named after the Italian scientist Alessandro Volta, who invented the first electric battery.

A *watt* is a measurement of the electrical power needed to keep an electric current flowing. If you look on the top of any light bulb you'll see a watts number printed on it. The amount of electric current your household uses is measured in kilowatts,

Scottish mechanical engineer James Watt
(1736–1819), inventor of the condensing
steam engine. The watt, a measure of
electrical power, is named after him.

or thousands of watts. Your electric meter shows how many kilowatts of electricity you use every month. Watts were named after James Watt, the Scottish scientist who invented the steam engine.

When the current is on, volts push amperes of electricity along a wire. We say that the wire is a conductor of electricity. The amount of electricity that the wire conducts when the current is on is measured in watts. The formula for this is: volts × amperes = watts.

A *coulomb* (koo-LOM) is the unit that measures the amount of electricity that passes a certain point in the conductor in a certain time. The coulomb was named after the French physicist Charles A. de Coulomb.

A *farad* is the unit of capacity in electricity—how much stored electricity anything will hold. It gets its name from Michael Faraday, who built the first electric generator.

MEASURING LIGHT

Like heat, light is also energy. Light travels in waves. An *angstrom* is the unit used for measuring wavelengths of light. An angstrom is a very small measurement, 1/250 of a millionth of an inch. In the metric system you would call it a decimillimicrometer. You can see why angstrom is simpler. The angstrom was named after the Swedish astronomer Anders Angstrom, who mapped the various kinds of light in the solar spectrum.

Candle power is a standard measurement for the brightness of light. It is the light given off by the flame of a candle of a definite size, shape, type of tallow, and wick. This standard was set by international agreement. If you put a surface 1 foot away from that candle, the brightness of the light falling on that surface is measured in *foot-candles*.

The amount of light falling on the surface is measured in *lumens*. You might find a lumens number on your light bulb, too.

ONE MEASUREMENT
FOR TIME
AND DISTANCE

A *light-year* is the distance light can travel in one year. It is a measurement of both time and distance. Since light travels at the enormous speed of 186,000 miles a second, a light-year is a huge distance, 6 million million miles (9.5 million million kilometers).

Light-years are used to measure the distances to the stars. Most stars in our galaxy are more than 100 light-years from earth.

Inside the solar system the distances are smaller, though by earth standards they are still quite big. The distance from the earth to the sun is 93 million miles, which is a unit of measurement called the *astronomical unit*, or 1 AU. The sun is 1 AU from earth. It's 1/3 of an AU from Mercury and 39 AU from Pluto, the outermost planet.

MAKING MAPS —— AND CHARTS ——

Maps and charts depend on accurate measurements of the earth's surface. Maps usually show area, locations, shapes, heights, and distances on land. The maps we call charts show coastlines, islands, water depths, currents, and other features sailors need to know when they are navigating on the sea or along lakes and rivers.

The oldest known map in existence was made on a clay tablet in Babylon, in about 3000 B.C. In the fifth century B.C., the Greeks tried to make a map of the world, but since they could only imagine what the world was like, the map didn't have much to do with geography.

In the first century A.D., the Greek mathematician and philosopher Ptolemy wrote his *Geographia*. Like all educated Greeks who had observed the curved shadow of the earth on the moon, he knew that the earth was a sphere, and he struggled with the puzzle of how to make a map of the round earth on a flat surface. It was Ptolemy who introduced the idea of latitude and longitude to locate places and positions on the earth, but his work was lost for almost 1,500 years.

Over the centuries the great explorers made many maps of their voyages, but modern mapmaking really began in the sixteenth century, when Gerhardus Mercator came up with the first way to show the round earth on a flat page. Today, there are a number of ways to do this, but no way is completely accurate. Ways of showing the earth on maps are called *projections.* Mapmakers choose one way or another, depending on the area they want to show.

Whether they are mapping the land or the sea, all geographers divide the earth into imaginary wedges so they can estimate distances and locations more easily. They use something called *circular measure.* Circular measure is based on the circle of the equator, but you can see how it works from any circle. A circle can be divided into 360 parts, called *degrees.* These degrees are like 360 thin wedges in a pie.

The practice of dividing a circle into degrees is one of the oldest in the world. The Babylonians did it first. Since they reckoned the year as 360 days, and they observed that a year was a circle of the seasons and the stars, they divided circles into 360 parts, too. This way of dividing a circle hasn't

A sixteenth-century map

changed in the thousands of years since the Babylonians did it.

A degree is fairly big as far as distance around the earth goes, so each degree is divided into 60 parts called *minutes*. Each minute is further divided into 60 *seconds*. Seconds are very small wedges in the pie of the earth's circle. These minutes and seconds of distance are different from the minutes and seconds of time, but they are related.

TIME AND DISTANCE

The 360-degree circle around the earth at the equator can be divided by the number of hours in a day, because the earth turns the full 360 degrees every twenty-four hours. The earth turns 15 degrees every hour, or 1 degree of distance every four minutes of time.

Every minute of distance around the circle is equal to one *nautical mile*, which is 1.1515 statute, or land, miles.

There are two kinds of degrees—degrees of *longitude* and degrees of *latitude*.

Degrees of longitude are measured by *meridians*, which are circles drawn around the earth from pole to pole, the way you would segment an orange. All meridians meet at the North and South Poles. Measurements start at Greenwich, England, which is called the *Prime Meridian*. The Prime Meridian is 0°. Degrees of longitude are measured in degrees east and west, up to 180°.

Parallels (lines) of latitude are drawn around the earth the way you would make flat slices in an apple. They are measured in degrees north and south of the equator, which is considered 0°. The latitude at each pole is 90°, north or south.

The map that sailors use is called a *chart*. No good sailor sails into unfamiliar water without a chart, even if that water is close to home port. There might be rocks just below the surface. There might be a bridge that is too low at certain tides. The current may be dangerously strong. All these things are marked on the chart. Distances on a chart are measured in nautical miles.

Nautical chart, with distances measured in nautical miles. Soundings are measured in feet at mean low water.

Depths of water are measured in feet or *fathoms*—the charts tell which. The fathom was an early measurement. It was 6 feet, the length to which a sailor could extend his arms sideways. This was an easy way to measure the cord that was used to take depth soundings. The depths given on a chart are measured at *mean low water,* which means average low tide. This is safer than measuring the depth at high tide, because hidden rocks or shoals are nearer to the surface when the tide is low.

Heights of things above the surface of the water are also shown on a navigation chart. They are measured in feet at *mean high water,* or high tide. If your boat has a 30-foot mast, and the height of a bridge is given at 28 feet, you know that you won't be able to pass under it at high tide. Sailors carry tide and current tables, too. Currents—fast-moving water—are measured in *knots.*

Buoys marking the entrance to a harbor or channel are numbered on charts. Number 1 is the buoy always the farthest out to sea. Going into a harbor, odd numbered buoys are always on the boat's left, or *port side,* while even numbered ones are on the boat's right, or *starboard side.* The safe channel is between them.

Lights at sea and lighthouses have their own pattern of flashes. Charts show the number of seconds between flashes.

All maps, whether they are land maps or charts of coastlines, plans for new roads or waterways, or plans of a city or a single piece of property, are made by *surveying.* Surveying is a science of measurement.

A surveyor at work

Surveying isn't done only once, then forgotten. Land may be surveyed first by explorers, then by settlers, then again for a different reason. At one time land surveys were done by people on foot, using simple instruments. Now, the most accurate surveys are done by satellites.

WAYS OF MEASURING

For determining distance, all surveys depend on linear measurement. If an area is difficult to measure directly, surveyors can measure it using angles and geometry. If the surveyors know the length of one distance, the task is easy. They divide the land to be measured into a triangle, with the distance they know as the *base*. Then they decide on some object they can see in the distance as the far point, called the *apex* of the triangle. They "sight" on this point with their instruments and, using an instrument called a theodolite (the-ODD-oh-lite), measure the angles at each end of the base. Then they use the rules of geometry to figure out the distances between each end of the base and the apex.

The measurement of the base must be exact. A mistake of one millionth of a part would make all the other figures wrong.

There are several ways of measuring the base. Sometimes the distance is measured with steel tapes 300 feet long and 3/8 of an inch wide. The tapes may be hung over trestles or laid along the ground. These same tapes divided into meters are used for surveying coastlines, rivers, and lakes.

Around 300 B.C., the Greeks surveyed their coast-line using a knotted floating line for a tape.

Sometimes, instead of a tape, surveyors use a chain. A chain is made of a hundred pieces of wire bent into links, each 7.92 inches long. A *survey-or's chain,* or *Gunter's chain,* is 66 feet long.

Surveyors use engineer's chains for surveying, too. They are 100 feet long with 1-foot links. The first foot is divided into fractions so that lengths of less than a foot can be measured exactly.

The ancient Egyptians were probably the first people to survey land accurately. Tomb paintings show two men using a chain to survey a field of corn. The oldest method of making a map involved measuring the ground directly with a chain, rope, or tape of a precise length.

On almost every map there is a distance scale. This shows how many miles or kilometers of actual distance each inch on the map represents. A large-scale map might show only a small area; maybe an inch would represent a mile. A small-scale map, on which an inch might represent 100 or 500 miles or more, would not show much detail.

MEASURING AREA

Although the Babylonians divided time into exact intervals and invented circular measurement, it appears that they never discovered that they could calculate area by multiplying length times width.

An important measurement of land area is the *acre.* An acre was originally the amount of land a yoke of oxen could plow in a day. Naturally, this figure varied a lot, depending on whether the farmer—and the oxen—were lazy or ambitious. Finally, Henry VIII of England made the acre an exact size. It was the area of a piece of land 40 measuring rods long by 40 rods broad. During the Middle Ages, the length of a rod was determined by lining up sixteen men outside of church on Sunday morning and measuring the combined length of all their left feet.

Rods were among the earliest standards of length. The Romans used 10-foot rods, with each foot a little over 13 inches long. Now a rod is 15½ feet, or 5½ yards, as it was in King Henry's day. Sometimes a rod is called a *pole.*

Thus, the area of an acre became, and still is, 160 square rods, or 4,840 square yards. A piece of land 200 feet by 200 feet is really an acre.

The unit of land measurement in the metric system is the *hectare,* which is 10,000 square meters, or 2.47 acres.

MEASURING DISTANCE

A *mile* is another measurement that has come down to us from the Romans. It was originally 1,000 passus (or paces). The passus was a Roman measure 5 feet long, the distance covered by a complete step. The mile stayed at 5,000 feet until about 1500, when it was changed to 5,280 feet. This made surveying land easier because the furlong, the most common measure of distance at that time, could then be divided into a mile eight times. About seventy-five years later Queen Elizabeth I established by law the length of a mile. Sometimes this 5,280-foot mile is called a *statute mile* or a *land mile*. In many places the use of the mile has been replaced by the metric system's kilometer. A kilometer is about 5/8 of a mile.

A *nautical mile* is 1.1515 land miles—1/21,600 of the great circle of the earth, a minute of circular measurement.

A *furlong* is 1/8 of a mile. At first it was the length of a furrow, the narrow groove that a plow digs in a field. The furlong is still used as a distance in horse races.

The *league* was an ancient Gallic measurement of distance that has varied in different times and in different countries from about 2½ to 4½ miles. Today we figure a league at 3 miles. If you traveled 20,000 leagues under the sea you would travel 60,000 miles, more than twice the distance around the earth. A *square league* is a 3-mile by 3-mile square, which is 9 square miles or 5,760 acres.

────────── **MEASURING A TOWN** ──────────

A *township* is a measure of area, 36 square miles. In the early days townships were marked off as convenient ways to divide large areas of land. Often a real town, with its own local government, grew up in a township.

A *block* is a varying unit of measure. It is land divided for the convenience of builders, with streets on all four sides. A usual city block is a little less than 265 feet long. But in the state of Texas a block is a piece of land at least a mile square.

ROAD MEASUREMENTS

Grade is a measurement of the slope of a road from a level surface. The slope can be expressed in different ways. Sometimes it is measured in degrees. A road rising at an angle of 15 degrees has a 15-degree grade. Sometimes grade is expressed in feet per 100 feet or feet per mile. Sometimes it is expressed as a percentage. A 10 percent grade would rise 10 feet for every 100 feet of its length.

A well-graded road is a feat of modern engineering, but the ancient Romans also graded their roads so well that they must have used surveying instruments.

MAPPING FROM THE SKY

To map the oceans and the continents, continuous series of pictures from satellites and aircraft are combined with measurements taken on the ground. Distance errors between continents are now less than 10 meters, thanks to geodetic (gee-oh-DET-ik) satellites that survey the earth from space.

THE
WEATHER

Long before there were any instruments at all, people had ways to predict the weather. Of course, they could never be sure what the weather would be. (Even today, with all kinds of high-tech instruments, we still can't be sure, but we can make better guesses.)

Then, in 1593, Galileo Galilei invented the thermometer. In 1643, Evangelista Torricelli invented the barometer. In 1714, Gabriel Fahrenheit invented the mercury thermometer and fixed a scale of temperature. And in 1742, Anders Celsius invented the centigrade thermometer.

Now there were scientific ways of measuring the weather and of using these measurements to predict what was coming. To tell you how hot or cold it is, there's the thermometer. But that doesn't tell you what may be coming. One of the best instruments for that is the barometer.

Left to right: hygrometer,
thermometer, and barometer.

MEASURING ATMOSPHERIC PRESSURE

The *barometer* measures atmospheric pressure, which is the weight of the atmosphere. Air presses down on everything on earth all the time. Because there are so many miles of air pushing down, this pressure is great. At sea level there are about 15 pounds of air pressing down on every square inch of matter.

Atmospheric pressure changes with the weather. If there is a mass of warm air high over an area, the pressure is low because warm air is relatively light. Cold air is heavier, so the air pressure is increased. Light, warm air holds much more moisture than cold air, so when the pressure is low it usually means that rain is coming. The lower the pressure, the bigger the storm.

When the pressure is high, the weather will probably be fair. Air pressure is measured in *millibars*. A millibar is 1/1000 of a *bar*, the standard unit for measuring air pressure.

Meterologists have special maps that tell them in more detail what the weather conditions are and what to expect. You can probably see a similar map in your daily newspaper. High and low pressure areas are marked on the map, and around them are lines called *isobars*. Isobars connect areas where the atmospheric pressure is the same. The closer together the isobars are, the faster the wind is moving. Isobars on a weather map show both the speed and the direction of the wind. Winds move the weather.

Sometimes, in winter, the weather report gives the wind chill factor in addition to the temperature. The wind chill factor is a combination of the temperature and the wind. If it's cold *and* windy, the air temperature may be 20°F, but a wind of 20 mph will make you lose body heat, so the temperature feels like −10°F.

MEASURING THE WIND

The speed, or velocity, of the wind near the ground is measured by an instrument called an *anemometer*. The anemometer's cups catch the wind, which spins the anemometer, turning the shaft connected to a speedometer. The speedometer shows the wind speed in miles per hour. Higher in the

THE BEAUFORT WIND SCALE

Beaufort Scale Number	Wind Description	Miles Per Hour	Wind Effect	Beaufort Symbol, Used On Weather Maps
0	calm	0–1	smoke goes straight up	
1	light air	2–3	smoke drifts in wind direction	
2	slight breeze	4–7	weathervanes turn, flags flutter, leaves move	
3	gentle breeze	8–12	flags blow out, small branches move	
4	moderate breeze	13–18	dust and papers blow around	
5	fresh breeze	19–24	small trees bend; whitecaps on water	

No.	Name	Speed	Description	
6	strong breeze (or wind)	25–31	large branches move, telephone wires whistle, umbrellas turn inside out, waves get big, whitecaps foam	
7	moderate gale (or high wind)	32–38	whole trees move; you have to lean against the wind to walk	
8	fresh gale	39–46	small branches break off trees	
9	strong gale	47–54	signs and TV antennas may blow down, shingles blow off, awnings rip	
10	whole gale	55–63	trees fall; wires and light structures down	
11	storm	64–75	widespread damage	
12	hurricane	over 75	disaster; countryside is devastated	

atmosphere, balloons with instruments attached measure wind speeds.

In 1805, a wind speed scale was invented by a British scientist, Rear Admiral Sir Francis Beaufort. The Beaufort wind scale also describes the nature of the wind at different speeds.

———————— MEASURING HUMIDITY ————————

The measurement of the amount of moisture in the air is called *relative humidity*. In a weather report, this is usually given as a percentage. The percentage is based on how much moisture the air could hold at the present temperature in relation to the current amount of moisture. Since the air can hold 100 percent before it starts to rain, a humidity of 50 percent means that the air is holding half the water vapor it can. The instrument that measures the moisture in the air is called a *psychrometer* (si-CROM-et-er).

Rainfall and snowfall are measured in inches. If a fall covers the surface of the ground to a depth of one inch, or fills a measuring device called a gauge to a depth of one inch, the weather report says that an inch of rain or snow has fallen. Gauges for measuring rain and snow depths are simply big cans with scales of inches marked on the inside walls.

Modern weather bureaus now use electronics and computers to forecast the weather. *Transmissionmeters* measure visibility. *Ceilometers* measure the height of clouds. A *telepsychronometer* measures humidity. Balloons have *radiosondes* to

measure temperature, relative humidity, atmospheric pressure, and wind speeds aloft. Sometimes *radar* can spot big storms on the way. *Satellites* photograph weather conditions around the
globe. Computers then take all this information plus
past weather data and use it to predict the coming
weather.

MEASURING
TIME

It has always been important to have a way of measuring time, but finding one hasn't been easy. Time can't be held in a container, lifted onto a scale, or measured with a stick.

The first way of measuring time was to keep a record of the repetition of natural events. From sunrise to sunrise was a period that could be measured. So was from one full moon to the next and one spring flowering to the next. Every repetition of a familiar event became a way of reckoning time. American Indians counted a year from one winter to the next, or one summer to the next. They counted months from full moon to full moon. They counted a day from one sleep to the next.

Gradually, people learned that the sun and the moon were the best timekeepers for the time periods we call days, months, and years. They didn't really understand what was happening over their heads, but the system they used worked.

A YEAR

Our *year* is the time the earth takes to orbit the sun. There are several ways to reckon a year.

The sidereal (sy-DEER-ee-al) year is determined by the changing positions of the stars. It's the method scientists use because it's the most precise. However, because it's also the most complicated way to figure, the rest of us generally use a different way of measuring.

We start at the moment when the sun's center crosses an imaginary line in space, drawn from the earth's equator. If you live in the northern hemisphere, the sun seems to be traveling north, toward you. When the sun crosses this imaginary line, day and night are equal all over the world. This moment is called the *vernal,* or *spring, equinox,* and is the beginning of spring.

Long ago, people actually started their year about the time of the spring equinox, when plants began to bloom again after winter. It wasn't until the beginning of the seventeenth century that they began to reckon the new year from January 1.

In the fall, the sun crosses the line again. If you live in the northern hemisphere, it seems to be going away from you. Day and night are equal again. This moment is called the *autumnal equinox.*

A year measured by the spring or by the autumnal equinox is called the astronomical, equinoctial, natural, or solar year. It is 365 days, 5 hours, 48 minutes, and 45.7 seconds long. The extra hours, minutes, and seconds are lumped together every four years to make the additional day we have in leap year.

TIME SCALE OF EARTH HISTORY

Time Scale	ERAS	Duration of Periods	PERIODS		DOMINANT ANIMAL LIFE
10 20 40 60 80	**CENOZOIC** 70 MILLION YEARS DURATION		Quaternary	Recent Pleistocene	Man
		70	Tertiary	EPOCHS: Pliocene Miocene Oligocene Eocene Paleocene	Mammals
100	**MESOZOIC** 120 MILLION YEARS DURATION	50	Cretaceous		
150		35	Jurassic		
		35	Triassic		Dinosaurs
200	**PALEOZOIC** 350 MILLION YEARS DURATION	25	Permian		
		20	Pennsylvanian		
250		30	Mississipian		Primitive reptiles
300		65	Devonian		Amphibians
350		35	Silurian		Fishes
400		75	Ordovician		
450					Invertebrates
500		90	Cambrian		
Figures in millions of years	**PROTEROZOIC** **ARCHAEOZOIC**	Figures in millions of years	1500 million years duration		Beginnings of life

Only during the last 500,000,000 years have plants and animals produced hard parts capable of being fossilized. This is a simplified chart of that quarter of the earth's history.

Time scale of the last 2 billion years of Earth's history

Ten years are called a *decade*, a hundred years are called a *century*, and a thousand years are called a *millennium*.

Geologic time is the time scale of the history of the earth. The largest divisions of geologic time are called *eras*. Eras are at least millions of years long.

A MONTH

The month was the earliest accurate division of time because it was figured from new moon to new moon—29½ days. This time period is called a *lunar month*, and at first the year was divided into twelve lunar months. But this didn't work well because figuring just twelve lunar months to a year leaves eleven days over if you're calculating a year by the earth's revolution around the sun. If those eleven days were used to start a new month, soon the year would be all mixed up, with no regular events governing it. The lunar month was fixed by the moon, the year was fixed by the sun, and they had no relation to each other. One had to be abandoned.

In the year 46 B.C., Julius Caesar abolished the use of the lunar year and added an extra day every four years to the solar year of 365 days. The twelve months are based roughly on the lunar months, but they aren't equal in length because later Roman rulers subtracted days from certain months and added them to other, more favored ones.

A WEEK

The seven-day week has no real connection with the movement of the sun and the moon, though the four-week month might have started as a division that represented the four quarters of the moon. Two weeks are called a *fortnight*, short for fourteen nights.

The seven days were probably named after the seven "planets" that were known to the ancient world. The bodies themselves were named after important gods. Sunday is the sun's day. Monday is the moon's day. Tuesday is Mars's day. (The Saxons called Mars *Tiw.*) Wednesday is Wodin's day. (Wodin was the Saxon name for Jupiter.) Thursday is Thor's day. (Thor wasn't a planet but the god of thunder.) Friday is dedicated to Venus, whom the Saxons called *Frigg.* And Saturday is Saturn's day. We still use the Saxon, or old English, names instead of the Latin names for the gods.

A DAY

The length of a day is fixed by the earth's rotation on its axis. As the earth turns, the sun seems to cross the various meridians, the imaginary lines drawn from pole to pole that divide the earth's surface. When the sun crosses any particular meridian again, a day has passed.

At different times of the year, the length of a day seems to vary. There are more hours of light or darkness because the positions of the earth and the sun are changing. However, to make timekeeping easier, we pretend that the sun always moves in the same path, midway between the points where the days are longest and shortest, and we reckon our day on that. We call this the *mean solar day.* "Mean" means average.

The moment when the sun crosses the meridian is noon. The sun is directly overhead. This would make the time different every few miles, so by international agreement the earth is divided into twenty-four time zones. Zones next to each other have a time difference of one hour.

When it is midnight at a particular place, a new day begins. This new day starts first at the meridian in the Pacific Ocean, halfway around the world from the meridian at Greenwich, England (the *Prime Meridian*). All over the world, time is measured from the Prime Meridian.

The place where the new day starts is called the *International Date Line.* When Monday starts at the International Date Line, it is still Sunday in the rest of the world.

In ancient times, days were reckoned from dawn to dawn in some places, from dusk to dusk in others. Today, a new day starts at midnight everywhere.

─────────────── **AN HOUR** ───────────────

An hour is a twenty-fourth part of the mean solar day. Hours are simply a convenient way of dividing a day. There is no natural division of time that makes an hour the length it is.

In some places, people divide a day into two

12-hour halves. The half before the sun crosses the meridian at noon is called A.M., or *ante merid-ian*. (*Ante* means "before.") After noon is P.M., short for *post meridian*. (*Post* means "after.") In other places, hours are numbered straight through from 1 to 24. This twenty-four-hour clock is also used by the military services. Aboard ships, the day is divided into six "watches" of four hours each. Bells tell the sailors what time it is: one bell for the first half hour of the watch, all the way up to eight bells for the last; then they start over.

The sundial was the first instrument for mea-suring time. The early sundial was simply an up-right stick that cast a shadow on the ground. A later sundial was a hollow half bowl with a bead on its edge, at the center. As the sun crossed the sky, the shadow of the bead moved across the bowl. The bowl was divided into twelve equal parts called *hours*. The length of the hour varied with the sea-sons. This way of measuring hours by dividing the daylight into twelve parts was used for a thousand years.

A MINUTE AND SECOND

A minute is a sixtieth of an hour, and a second is a sixtieth of a minute. Both these measurements are convenient for dividing time. The ancient Ba-bylonians started these divisions, dividing many of their measurements into sixty parts. The Babyloni-ans used a water clock to reckon time. The water dripped from one jar to another, through a hole of a carefully calculated size. The time it took for the water to drip completely through was the length of a day. This clock was more accurate than any devised afterward for several thousand years.

Modern life runs on schedules. In manufacturing, many processes must be timed precisely. Parts on an assembly line must appear exactly when they are needed. China and cookies are both baked for a certain length of time. Paint is dried, canned and frozen foods are processed, and trains and traffic lights run on schedules. So do television and radio stations. Clocks are among the most important measuring tools ever invented. A clock with hands turns invisible time into a specific distance on the clock's face. If the clock is *digital,* a computer in the clock divides time into hours, minutes, and seconds. Electronic circuits in the clock make the numbers glow as they mark the passage of time.

People have always thought that time was constant, that it never changed, that a year was a year and a second a second, no matter what. Albert Einstein's theory of relativity states that this is not true. It says that the faster something is moving, the more time slows down for that moving thing. This could make a big difference in space travel, if we ever learn how to make spaceships that can travel at speeds close to the speed of light. Years on earth might only be weeks or months to the space travelers. There might be time to travel to the stars.

MEASURING SPEED
—AND DISTANCE—

When people first began moving from place to place, measuring distance and speed was a simple matter. You could walk to the sea if you started at daybreak. You got there at sunset. The distance to the sea was how far. From daybreak to sunset was the time it took.

ON THE WATER

On the water, if you had a boat with a sail and the wind was good, you could move faster than you could on land. Because seafarers could travel farther and faster than land travelers, for thousands of years goods and travelers moved by water whenever possible.

Even before they had any instruments, sailors had ways of measuring, some of which are still used today. One early measurement was a *fathom,* 6 feet. If a sailor measured off 6 fathoms of cord before the weight at the bottom of the cord hit the sea bottom alongside the ship, the water was 36 feet deep. Water depth is still measured in fathoms.

Today, instruments aboard ships send out sound waves to measure water depth. The time between the instant the sound waves leave the ship, bounce off the sea bottom, and return is recorded by a computer and automatically changed into fathoms or feet. The fathometer works continuously, recording the depth of the water through which the ship is passing.

One hundred fathoms make a cable's length. The usual length of a ship's cable is about 600 feet. In the U.S. Navy, though, a cable is 720 feet, or 120 fathoms. Ten cable lengths equal 1 nautical mile, which is 6,076.097 feet. Sixty nautical miles equal 1 degree at the equator.

A *knot* is the unit used to measure the speed at which ships travel. One knot is equal to 1 nautical mile an hour. If a ship is traveling at 20 knots, it is going 20 nautical miles an hour. Sailors never say, "twenty knots an hour," because that would be like saying, "twenty nautical miles an hour an hour."

Originally, a knot was a division in the ship's *log line*. This line was tied to a small log that kept the line afloat when it was thrown overboard and unreeled. The line was knotted at intervals, and the knots were in the same proportion to a mile that 28 seconds are to an hour, so they were about 47 feet apart. The number of knots that ran off a reel of line in 28 seconds was the number of nautical miles the ship was traveling in an hour.

Now, even small pleasure boats often have instruments that show the speed of the ship through the water. This speed varies from the engine speed because different winds or currents push the boat faster or slower. Some instruments show how far it is to the boat's next mark. Some even show the boat's latitude and longitude.

In the earliest days, sailors reckoned their position and direction by the positions of the sun in the daytime and the stars at night. Before they had instruments to help them, very few sailors dared to travel out of sight of land for more than a few hours. If the compass hadn't been invented, Columbus would never have come in search of the Indies. (The Chinese were using a kind of compass on land long before European sailors took it to sea starting in the fourteenth century.)

ON THE LAND

On land, oxcarts were probably the first big improvement in moving faster. (They didn't move as fast as runners in relay, but that speed was reserved for kings and generals who had important messages to send.) And since horses were faster than oxen, using them was the next big improvement. You could ride a horse or hitch it to a vehicle. In the seventeenth century, if you took a trip by fast coach, you might travel 45 miles in a day. It would take thirteen or fourteen days to travel 500 miles.

In the nineteenth century, the steam engine was invented, and in 1829 an engine called the "Rocket" set a record speed of 29 miles per hour (mph).

Many people thought that the human body would not be able to stand the strain of going much faster.

Then came the automobile. Some early cars ran on steam, some on electricity, and some on gasoline. We picture them as being slow, but in 1908 a Stanley Steamer set a land speed record of 127.66 mph.

Modern cars have instruments and computers that are constantly measuring and regulating. They report some things to the car itself, and some to the driver, on the dashboard.

The *speedometer* measures how fast the car is going, in miles per hour or kilometers per hour, or both. The *odometer* measures the mileage—the total mileage or the mileage for one trip. The *fuel gauge* measures the amount of gas in the tank. In some cars a computer calculates how many miles to the gallon the car is getting. Other gauges signal oil temperature, engine temperature, and any problems in the engine.

IN THE AIR

The first airplane flew at the speed of 31 miles per hour. Gradually, plane speeds increased until they reached a speed of almost 750 mph. Then a wall stood in the way—a wall of sound. Scientists called this the *sound barrier*. Planes couldn't pass through it.

Sound waves travel at about 742 miles an hour. As long as the plane is going slower than that, the waves move out, away from the plane. But when a plane was moving at the speed of sound, all those bunched up waves of air, carrying the sound, couldn't get ahead of it. They piled up in front of the plane, and it seemed as if the plane were really crashing into something. Designers had to find new shapes for planes that would enable them to cut through the sound barrier.

Supersonic (which means "faster than sound") planes look different. They have long, sharp noses and swept-back wings. They slice through the sound barrier instead of bumping into it. Once they are through (there is a loud bang, called a *sonic boom,* when that happens), the planes can go faster and faster with no noise because the sound is always behind them.

The speed of sound is called *mach 1.* Twice the speed of sound is mach 2, and so on. The word

Aviators use a wide array of instruments

comes from the Austrian physicist, Ernst Mach, who almost a hundred years ago studied the nature of shock waves.

Instruments in a plane measure more than air speed. They also measure how fast the plane is climbing or going down. A *tachometer* shows how fast the engine is turning. One *altimeter* shows how high above sea level the plane is and another shows how high it is above the land directly below the plane. Other dials show exactly where the plane is at any moment. Airliners and jets have hundreds of instruments.

IN SPACE

Everything about space is bigger or faster or hotter or colder or farther than anything on earth. Space itself is so immense that we can't really imagine it. Some stars are so far away that it takes billions of years for their light to reach us. There are more stars in our galaxy than we can count. And there are probably more galaxies than there are stars in our galaxy. Some scientists say that the number of stars in the galaxies is infinite. This means that they go on forever. You cannot count an infinite number of anything. Infinity is an idea, not a number.

Scientists who work with such enormous numbers use a kind of special number called an *exponent*. An exponent stands for how many times a number is multiplied by itself. For example, if you want to write the number 10 billion, instead of writing 10,000,000,000 you can write 10^{10}.

Distances in space are measured in light-years—the distance light travels in a year—6 million million miles. Some distances in space are measured in billions of light-years. Distances like that can only be gauged by telescopes. No space vehicle has gone much beyond our own solar system—a very small distance even when compared to the width of our galaxy.

For getting away from earth at all, people had to find a way to overcome the force of gravity. Gravity is the pull of the earth on everything on and around it. The measurement for the force of gravity is written as g. At the earth's surface, there is a pull of 1g on you. This is equal to your weight. Blasting off in a rocket or coming back to earth causes the g force to increase. If there is a pull of 2g on you, your weight doubles. If you weigh 100 pounds, at 2g you would weigh 200, at 5g you would weigh 500.

The power in the engines that drive a rocket is called *thrust*. Thrust is measured in pounds. The combined thrust of a number of huge rocket engines may be in the millions of pounds.

The speed that is needed to escape from the earth's gravity is called *escape velocity*. Escape velocity from earth is 25,000 miles an hour.

A satellite's orbit is the path the satellite travels around the earth. The satellite's distance from

**Liftoff of the *Gemini IV*.
Rockets must overcome
the force of gravity in
order to enter space.**

the earth may change as the satellite moves along in its orbit. The farthest point in the orbit is called the *apogee height*. The closest point is called the *perigee height*. These distances are measured in miles or kilometers. The length of time it takes for a satellite to complete an orbit is called the satellite's *period*. The period is measured in minutes, hours, days, or years.

Scientists call the cycle of light and darkness the *diurnal cycle*. We call it day and night. In a satellite orbiting the earth, day and night are meaningless because light and darkness follow each other in minutes. Astronauts in orbit have to make up day and night schedules of their own, so they can eat and sleep regularly.

In space, radiation from the sun is very intense. Some of this radiation is in the form of cosmic ray particles, bits of atoms traveling at almost the speed of light. Their energy is measured in *electron volts*, from 100 million to 10 billion electron volts.

Radiation can also be measured in *curies*. Curies were named for Marie and Pierre Curie, who discovered radiation. Exposure to radiation is figured in *roentgens* per hour. (William Roentgen was the man who discovered X-rays.) A human could take an exposure of 0.2 or 0.3 roentgens for weeks without being harmed. But in some parts of space, instruments have monitored 10 roentgens.

On earth, people who work with radioactive materials wear monitor tags that show how much radiation they are being exposed to. If the monitor shows they have gone beyond a safe limit, they stop their work.

──COMMUNICATIONS──

──────── PRINTING ────────

There might not have been a way to measure signal fires or smoke signals, but the timing of drumbeats probably sent messages that hearers who knew the code could interpret. Greek soldiers sent messages by reflecting flashes of sunlight from their shields. Numbers and writing sent their own kinds of messages from the people who wrote them to the people who could read them. But there were probably no measurements related to writing itself until the eighth century, when the Chinese began printing from engraved wooden blocks.

Legend has it that the first movable type was invented by a Chinese woodcarver named Pi; a number of printing terms are named after him. The most important of these is the *pica*, a size of type that equals .166, or 1/6, of an inch. Pi's blocks represented the first time pictures or writing had

**A page from the earliest printed book
still in existence (China, 868 A.D.)**

ever been reproduced in any way except by hand.
It wasn't until the thirteenth century that people in
Europe began printing from wooden blocks. Then,
in the fifteenth century, Johannes Gutenberg invented the first movable type letters that could be
used on a printing press. That was the beginning
of modern printing.

The *point* is the standard unit of measure for
type size all over the world. It began as a French
measure that was later adopted by printers in other

countries because of their need for a simple way to compare different sizes of type. The system of measuring points began by taking the pica type, the most common type size, and dividing it into twelve parts called points. As said earlier, pica type was approximately 1/6 of an inch high, so each point was about 1/72 of an inch.

The point system of measuring is used for all type styles and was adopted by the U.S. Type Founders Association in 1886. But a great many printers were using it before it became official.

The height of the type determines its point size. All 12-point types, for example, will be the same height, even though their widths may vary a great deal. The type in this book is 11 points.

The *em* is one of the printer's most useful standards. An em is the portion of a line taken up by the letter M in whatever type is being used. An *en* is the width of the letter N and is half as wide as an em.

A pica was originally just a size of type 12 points high. Since a point is 1/72 of an inch high, a 12-point letter is 1/6 of an inch high, and that is the measurement of a pica. Column widths are most commonly measured in picas. Printers, book designers, writers, and other people who work with type have special rulers called *pica rules*. These have inches divided into sixths. A *nonpareil* (non-pah-RELL) is 6 points, or 1/12 of an inch.

Leading (LEDD-ing) is the white space between lines of type. It began as thin metal strips used to separate type lines. Leadings vary in thickness from 1/2 point, which is 1/144 of an inch, to 3 points, which is 1/24 of an inch. The most common is 2-point leading, but leadings can be put together to make wider spaces between lines. The leading in this book is 2 points. A printer would say that a book is set in "eleven on thirteen," which means that it is 11-point type set in a space 13 points deep.

Type size is figured in points, but in addition to the height of the letter, its width has a lot to do with the size the type appears to be. A type can be

STANDARD
CONDENSED
EXTRA CONDENSED
EXTENDED

The weight of a type is reckoned by the thickness of the lines that make up the letters. In weight a type might be

LIGHT FACE
MEDIUM
BOLD FACE
EXTRA BOLD

A *stick* of copy began as a composing stick, or narrow metal tray in which type was set. A *slug* of type is a line of type set in one piece.

A *ream* is 500 sheets of paper. A *quire* is 24 or 25 sheets.

A *pound* is the unit of measurement for the weight of paper. A printer might buy 10,000 pounds of 60-pound paper. Sixty pounds would be the weight of 500 sheets of a certain size.

There are different kinds of 60-, 80-, or 90-pound papers. Paper to be used for pages in a book may be entirely different from the jacket paper, though they could both be 60-pound papers. If you ask a printer to explain this to you, he or she would probably cover whole sheets of paper with figures, then say that it would take a book to really explain it. Ink is bought by the pound, too, but just by plain, ordinary pounds.

A *signature* is a section of a finished book that is folded and bound with other signatures to make the whole book. If you look at the top of this book you will see several signatures bound together. Each one is actually just one big printed sheet folded and cut into smaller pages.

PHOTOGRAPHY

Photographs certainly communicate. There's the familiar saying that one picture is worth a thousand words. Here are some important measurements in photography.

Focal length is the distance from the camera lens to the image on the film when the lens is focused at infinity. The word *image* is important here. Focal length is not the distance from the lens to the object being photographed but the distance from the lens to the image of the object on the film, behind the lens.

Focal length can be measured either in inches or in millimeters. A motion-picture camera, for example, may have a lens with a focal length of 2 inches, or 50 millimeters. Photographers change the lenses on their cameras to get different kinds of pictures. From the same distance a lens of one focal length will get everything in a scene, while the lens of another focal length will get a close-up of only one face. With a *zoom lens* a photographer can change the focal length to get both kinds of pictures with the same lens.

F-stop is the measure of the amount of light passing through the lens. When there is a lot of light, you change the f-stop to allow less light through to the film. Too much light makes the picture too light, or *overexposes* it. Every time the lens is closed 1 f-stop, the amount of light coming into the camera is reduced by half. The larger the number on the f-stop, the smaller the amount of light that comes in. F-stops usually run from 1.2, which lets in the most light, to 32, which lets in the least.

Shutter speed is the amount of time the shutter is open to allow light to fall on the film. The shutter lets light through to the lens. When cameras were first invented, the light had to come through for several minutes in order to expose the film. Now exposure is faster, so shutter speeds are faster, too. Shutter speeds are usually anywhere from 8 seconds to 1/1,200 of a second.

Camera films are rated by their sensitivity to light. The more sensitive the film is, the faster it is. Usually, film speed is indicated by an ASA (American Standards Association) number; the smaller the number, the slower the film is. Ratings start at ASA 25, the slowest. They then go from 64, 100, 200, 400, and 800 to 1250, the fastest film.

MOTION PICTURES

Moving pictures don't really move. The only thing that moves is the film. It moves past the lens of the camera as it is being exposed and past the lens of the projector as it is being shown.

Film is normally shot and projected at twenty-four frames a second. (A *frame* is a single picture.) Because the frames go by so fast, your eyes don't see the blank spaces between the pictures. Twenty-four frames a second is called *sound speed.*

When a scene is filmed at more than twenty-four frames a second but projected at the normal twenty-four frames, you see the scene in *slow motion.* For example, if an action is filmed at forty-eight frames a second and projected at twenty-four, it will take twice as long for the scene to go through the projector. It will be on the screen twice as long so the motion will seem slow. Sixty-four frames is very slow motion. Very, very slow motion, such as a berry falling into a cup of milk, for example, where you see the splash rising into a sort of crown, is filmed at 500 frames a second or more.

When scenes are filmed at less than twenty-four frames a second, the action seems to move fast. At twelve frames a second, it is very fast. At six frames a second it is superfast.

Stop motion might be one frame a second, one

frame an hour, or even one frame a day. If you are filming at one frame an hour, a day will go by in one second. Films that show clouds forming and moving across a landscape—or a flower growing, unfolding, blossoming, and dying—are made this way. Many of the commercials you see on television are filmed at superfast or ultraslow speeds.

Film sizes are measured in millimeters. The size refers to the width of the film. Super 8 and 8 mm films are used for home movies. Sixteen mm is a semi-professional size. It is also used for many documentaries. Thirty-five mm is theater size, for ordinary screens. Seventy mm is wide screen. Thirty-five mm film runs through the projector at ninety feet a minute.

——————— TELEVISION AND RADIO ———————

A picture appears on your television set, and sound comes out of your television or your radio, because electromagnetic waves have moved from one place to another. Electromagnetic waves move at the speed of light. One complete movement of an electromagnetic wave is called a *cycle*. A cycle is measured from the top of one wave to the top of the next. That measure is called a *wavelength*. The height of a wave is called its *amplitude*.

Electromagnetic waves come in assorted lengths. Radar waves are very short. Ultrahigh-frequency television waves (UHF) are a little longer, and the very-high-frequency TV waves (VHF) are still longer. Then come line-of-sight broadcasting waves—FM waves—the waves used for long-distance broadcasting, ordinary broadcasting, and finally the longest waves, which are almost a mile long.

Because electromagnetic waves move so fast, they are measured in kilocycles (a thousand cycles) a second. These are usually called *kilohertz*, after Gustav Hertz, a German physicist.

Frequency is the measurement of the number of cycles that form in a second. When you hear an announcement that a television or radio station is operating on a frequency of so many kilohertz, you know that the station is broadcasting that many thousands of waves a second.

Sound travels in waves, too, but sound waves are much slower than electromagnetic waves. Sound waves travel at only 742 miles an hour, and then they fade. Sound waves are changed into radio waves to be broadcast. Then, in your set, they are changed back into audio-frequency waves. That means that they are vibrating slowly enough to be heard. The loudness of sound is measured in *decibels.* A whisper is 10 decibels. Traffic is 70 decibels. Rock music is 80 decibels. A jet plane taking off is 100 decibels.

The picture on your TV screen is created by an electron beam that scans across the television picture tube and causes the chemicals on the screen to glow at different levels of brightness. The beam scans across the tube in straight lines, one below the other. In the United States there are 525 lines on the screen. New high-definition screens have 720 or more lines.

The lines that make up the picture are chang-

ing all the time. The beam of electrons in your re-
ceiver scans the screen, making new pictures thirty
times a second.

A television program may be live, on film, or
recorded electronically on magnetic tape. The tape
used in home TV camcorders is 8 mm, or 1/4 of an
inch. Professional tapes are measured in inches. A
tape may be 1/4 inch, 1/2 inch, 1 inch, or 2 inches
wide.

COMMUNICATIONS SATELLITES

The first communications satellite was *Echo*,
launched in 1960. *Echo* was a huge Mylar balloon,
about ten stories tall. Its orbit was about 150 miles
up. *Echo* was a passive satellite. It didn't do anything except act as a mirror to reflect radio signals
back to earth.

Telstar, launched in 1962, was the first active
satellite. It amplified signals and changed their
frequencies so that the signals being sent out
wouldn't interfere with the ones coming in. It pro-
vided television and telephone service. It rebroad-
cast news photographs.

Telstar was 3,000 miles above the earth. It or-
bited the earth nine times a day, going so fast that
its transmissions to any station on the ground were
very short.

Now, communications satellites are 22,300
miles above the earth. That distance puts them in
geosynchronous (gee-oh-SIN-cron-us) *orbit*. They
travel at the same speed as the earth, so they are

The *Telstar* communications satellite. Satellites circle the earth in geosynchronous orbit.

always in the same position over the earth. At that height the signals from only three satellites could transmit line-of-sight signals to almost every place on earth, but most countries and companies want their own satellites. Now there are so many satellites in geosynchronous orbit that there is almost a traffic jam out there.

A satellite receives signals, sorts them, amplifies them, and beams them to earth stations all over the world. The satellite device that receives the signals, amplifies and changes them, and re-broadcasts them is called a *transponder*. Communications satellites have twelve, twenty-four, or more transponders. A transponder can send out more than 92 million bits of information in a second to earth stations in different places. Sending signals from an earth station in space is called *up-linking*. Sending signals from a satellite to an earth station is called *down-linking*.

Today, the biggest measurement problem in communications is how to satisfy all the users of radio frequencies. More and more communications devices are being invented, and there's not enough room for them all. There are a limited number of usable bands. New ways of carrying messages, such as fiber optics and laser beams, are helping solve this problem.

COMPUTERS

Computers are great communicators. They communicate with people, with satellites, and with other computers. They measure, compare, and solve complex mathematical problems. They control complicated processes, keep track of millions of items, translate languages, break codes, and manage bank accounts. They make predictions, diagnose diseases, figure orbits, draw, and design.

Computers use basically four systems to do their work. Some use the *binary system*—two symbols, 0 and 1. Combinations of those two numerals make up all the letters and numbers we use. To the computer, 0 and 1 simply mean "off" and "on."

Some use the decimal system, ten numerals: 0123456789. Some use an octal, or base 8, system: 01234567. Some use a hexadecimal system: 0123456789ABCDEF.

Computers have their own units of measurement. The smallest unit is a *bit* (from *bi*nary dig*it*). Eight bits make up a *byte*. A byte is a single character of information—a letter, number, punctuation mark, or symbol.

A computer's memory is measured in thousands of bytes, or *kilobytes*. A million bytes is a *megabyte*.

Computers figure how much and how many, how big and how small, how fast and how far at speeds that would seem quite magical to those first humans who scratched their measurements on clay tablets.

TABLES OF ——WEIGHTS AND—— MEASURES

AVOIRDUPOIS WEIGHT

27 11/32 grains (*gr.*)	1 dram (*dr.*)
16 drams	1 ounce (*oz.*), 437 1/2 grains
16 ounces	1 pound (*lb.*), 256 drams, 7,000 grains
100 pounds	1 hundredweight (*cwt.*), 1,600 ounces
112 pounds	1 long hundredweight (*l. cwt.*)
20 hundredweight	1 ton (*tn.*), 2,000 pounds
20 long hundredweight	1 long ton (*l. tn.*), 2,240 pounds

TROY WEIGHT

24 grains (*gr.*)	1 pennyweight (*dwt.*)
20 pennyweights	1 ounce (*oz. t.*), 480 grains
12 ounces	1 pound (*lb. t.*), 240 pennyweights, 5,760 grains

APOTHECARIES' WEIGHT

20 grains (*gr.*)	1 scruple (*s. ap.* or Ә)
3 scruples	1 dram (*dr. ap.* or ӡ), 60 grains
8 drams	1 ounce (*oz. ap.* or ӡ̄), 24 scruples, 480 grains
12 ounces	1 pound (*lb. ap.* or ℔.), 96 drams, 288 scruples, 5,760 grains

LINEAR MEASURE

12 inches (*in.*)	1 foot (*ft.*)
3 feet	1 yard (*yd.*), 36 inches
5 1/2 yards	1 rod (*rd.*), 16 1/2 feet
40 rods	1 furlong (*fur.*), 220 yards, 660 feet
8 furlongs	1 statute (mile) *mi.*, 1,760 yards, 5,280 feet
3 miles	1 league (*l.*), 5,280 yards

SQUARE MEASURE

144 square inches (*sq. in.*)	1 square foot (*sq. ft.*)
9 square feet	1 square yard (*sq. yd.*), 1,296 square inches
30 1/4 square yards	1 square rod (*sq. rd.*), 272 1/4 square feet
160 square rods	1 acre (*A.*), 4,840 square yards
640 acres	1 square mile (*sq. mi.*), 3,097,600 square yards
36 square miles	1 township

CUBIC MEASURE

1,728 cubic inches (*cu. in.*)	1 cubic foot (*cu. ft.*)
27 cubic feet	1 cubic yard (*cu. yd.*)
144 cubic inches	1 board foot
128 cubic feet	1 cord

---------------- CHAIN MEASURE ----------------

Gunter's, or surveyor's, chain

7.92 inches (*in.*)	1 link (*li.*)
100 links	1 chain (*ch.*)
80 chains	1 mile (*mi.*)

Engineer's chain

12 inches	1 link
100 links	1 chain
52.8 chains	1 mile

---------------- SURVEYOR'S AREA MEASURE ----------------

625 square links (*sq. li.*)	1 square rod or square pole (*sq. p.*)
16 square rods	1 square chain (*sq. ch.*), surveyor's
10 square chains	1 acre (*A.*)
640 acres	1 square mile (*sq. mi.*)
36 square miles	1 township

---------------- LIQUID MEASURE ----------------

4 gills (*gi.*)	1 pint (*pt.*)
2 pints	1 quart (*qt.*), 8 gills
4 quarts	1 gallon (*gal.*), 8 pints, 32 gills
31 1/2 gallons	1 barrel (*bbl.*), 126 quarts
2 barrels	1 hogshead (*hhd.*), 63 gallons, 252 quarts

---------------- APOTHECARIES' FLUID MEASURE ----------------

60 minims (*min.* or ℥)	1 fluid dram (*fl. dr.* or f℥)
8 fluid drams	1 fluid ounce (*fl. oz.* or f℥), 480 minims
16 fluid ounces	1 pint (*o.*), 128 fluid drams, 7,680 minims
8 pints	1 gallon (*C.*), 128 fluid ounces, 1,024 fluid drams

———————————— DRY MEASURE ————————————

2 pints (*pt.*)	1 quart (*qt.*)
8 quarts	1 peck (*pk.*), 16 pints
4 pecks	1 bushel (*bu.*), 32 quarts, 64 pints
105 quarts	1 barrel (*bbl.*), dry measure, 7,056 cubic inches

———————————— CIRCULAR MEASURE ————————————

60 seconds (")	1 minute (')
60 minutes	1 degree (°)
90 degrees	1 quadrant (*quad.*)
4 quadrants	1 circle

———————————— NAUTICAL MEASURE ————————————

6 feet	1 fathom (*fath.*)
100 fathoms	1 cable's length (ordinary)
120 fathoms	1 cable's length (United States Navy)
10 cable's lengths	1 nautical mile
1 nautical mile	1.1515 statute miles
60 nautical miles	1 degree (*deg.* or °)

———————————— CONVERSION TABLE ————————————

Metric system into customary system and customary system into metric system. These values are very exact.

centimeter	0.3937 inch
meter	39.37 inches (exactly)
square centimeter	.1549997 square inch
square meter	1.195985 square yards
hectare	2.47104 acres
cubic meter	1.3079428 cubic yards
liter	.264178 gallon
liter	1.05671 liquid quarts

liter	.908102 dry quart
hectoliter	2.83782 bushels
gram	15.432356 grains
kilogram	2.204622341 pounds, avoirdupois
inch	2.540005 centimeters
yard	.9144018 meter
square inch	6.451626 square centimeters
square yard	.8361307 square meter
acre	.404687 hectare
cubic yard	.7645594 cubic meter
gallon	3.785332 liters
liquid quart	.946333 liter
dry quart	1.101198 liters
bushel	35.23833 liters
grain	.064798918 gram
pound, avoirdupois	.45359237 kilogram

INDEX